CO-007 S

A COMPLETE INTRODUCTION TO

BREEDING
AQUARIUM FISHES

A male Three-striped Croaking Gourami (Trichopsis schalleri) *usually builds the bubblenest under a broad leaf.*

Golden Dwarf Cichlid
(Nannacara anomala) guarding
the fry.

A COMPLETE INTRODUCTION TO
BREEDING
AQUARIUM FISHES

The male Blunthead Cichlid (Aequidens curviceps) *waits patiently as the female lays the eggs.*

—Dr. Herbert R. Axelrod—

PHOTOGRAPHY Aqua Life: 55 (upper); Dr. Herbert R. Axelrod: 13, 20, 53 (lower), 88 (upper); H. Azuma: 10, 75, 74; Dr. Warren E. Burgess: 13; E. A. Baumback: 53 (upper), 120 (lower); Wolfgang Bechtle: 49; Dr. W. Foersch: 121; S. Frank: 21 (upper), 31 (lower), 98 (upper); H. Franke: 77 (lower); Michael Gilroy: 17, 27; Dr. Harry Grier: 77, 115; H. Hansen: 99; J. Kadlec: 30, 31 (upper); Burkhard Kahl: 82 (upper), 113; Dr. H. H. Reichenbach-Klinke: 16; Al Liebetrau: 107; H. Petersmann: 12, 56, 57; H. J. Richter: 8, 9, 23, 26, 29, 33, 34, 39, 40, 43 (lower), 45 (upper), 46, 58, 59, 60, 61, 62 (upper), 67, 68, 69, 70, 72 (lower), 73, 79, 80 (lower), 81 82 (lower), 83, 84, 85, 86, 87, 88 (lower), 89, 90, 93, 94 (lower), 96, 97, 101 (lower), 102, 103, 104, 108 (upper), 109 (lower), 111, 112, 117, 119 (upper), 120 (upper); Husein Rofe: 52; Andre Roth: 91 (upper), 94 (upper), 106 (middle); Yohei Sakamoto: 47; Chuck Sanclers: 55 (lower); Dr. Edmund Schmdit: 54; A. Scott: 98; J. Vierke: 61; J. Voss: 65 (upper); Uwe Werner: 12, 28; Peter Wong: 41; R. Zukal: 11, 21, 25, 30, 32, 42, 43 (upper), 48 (lower), 62 (lower), 63, 72 (upper), 91 (lower), 92, 100 (upper), 101 (upper), 109 (upper), 114, 116, 119 (lower), 112 (upper).

Distributed in the UNITED STATES by T.F.H. Publications, Inc., 211 West Sylvania Avenue, Neptune City, NJ 07753; in CANADA to the Pet Trade by H & L Pet Supplies Inc., 27 Kingston Crescent, Kitchener, Ontario N2B 2T6; Rolf C. Hagen Ltd., 3225 Sartelon Street, Montreal 382 Quebec; in CANADA to the Book Trade by Macmillan of Canada (A Division of Canada Publishing Corporation), 164 Commander Boulevard, Agincourt, Ontario M1S 3C7; in ENGLAND by T.F.H. Publications Limited, 4 Kier Park, Ascot, Berkshire SL5 7DS; in AUSTRALIA AND THE SOUTH PACIFIC by T.F.H. (Australia) Pty. Ltd., Box 149, Brookvale 2100 N.S.W., Australia; in NEW ZEALAND by Ross Haines & Son, Ltd., 18 Monmouth Street, Grey Lynn, Auckland 2 New Zealand; in SINGAPORE AND MALAYSIA by MPH Distributors (S) Pte., Ltd., 601 Sims Drive, #03/07/21, Singapore 1438; in the PHILIPPINES by Bio-Research, 5 Lippay Street, San Lorenzo Village, Makati Rizal; in SOUTH AFRICA by Multipet Pty. Ltd., 30 Turners Avenue, Durban 4001. Published by T.F.H. Publications Inc. Manufactured in the United States of America by T.F.H. Publications, Inc.

CONTENTS

Introduction

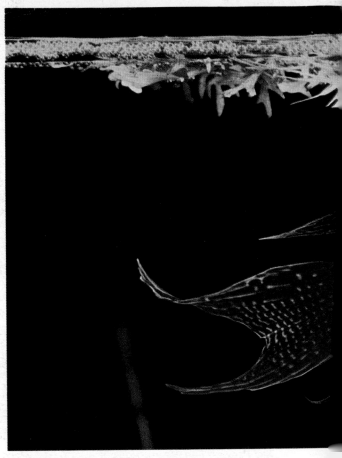

It has long been the contention of many scientists that most fishes merely lay their eggs whenever and wherever a ripe female meets an active male. They assume that few fishes exhibit any form of parental or nesting behavior and that the main classifications of fishes have little correlation with breeding habits. I do not agree.

If the small fishes which we call "tropical aquarium fishes" are any sample of the 30,000 known living fishes, then about 40 percent of them exhibit some degree of post-spawning recognition of their responsibility to the preservation of the species.

The Cichlids, for example, spawn in a remarkably similar fashion. They lay large eggs. The eggs are more or less adhesive. The parents, and normally there is only a single male and a single female involved, engage in a pre-spawning association which might be called a "courtship," but which certainly serves as a minimum of a 24-hour get-together (some fishes will spawn with any random encounter with the opposite sex in minutes after their meeting). The number of Cichlid eggs will usually be between 200 and 1,000. The eggs will usually hatch in about three days at 72° F. One of the parents, and in some cases both parents, are *necessary* for the incubation of the eggs and the feeding and

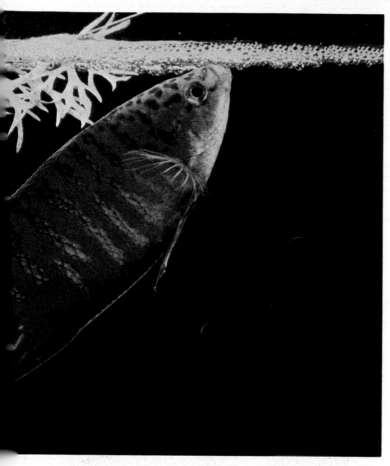

This Paradise Fish (Macropodus opercularis) *has utilized a cluster of* Riccia fluitans, *a common floating water plant, in building his bubblenest.*

protection of the fry. Some Cichlids are mouthbrooders, incubating the eggs and caring for the fry in their mouths. Some merely herd their fry about and protect them from predators as best they can. But all are "devoted" parents.

Experiments made by hundreds of fish breeders have proved that many Cichlid spawns can be removed from the parents and the young reared artificially in nearly every instance, even with *Symphysodon* where the young normally eat the slime secretion from their parents' body. But in these cases a human has become the foster parent, for should the Cichlid parents desert their spawn in nature, other fishes would surely devour the eggs or young before they had a chance to fend for themselves.

Many African Cichlids are mouthbrooders and we find a few odd South American Cichlids with similar behavior. We also find other fishes *(Osteoglossum)* which are not related to Cichlids at all, which also incubate their eggs orally. So we certainly are not implying that fishes should be classified according to their spawning habits...but neither should their spawning habits be ignored.

With the exception of the fishes in the genus *Copella,* fishes in the same genus can usually be expected to spawn in a similar manner and aquarists should attempt to supply similar breeding "set-ups" to fishes of the same genus. This is how the professional usually succeeds in spawning a "new" fish. He determines the family to which it belongs, tries to associate its observable living habits with other fishes he knows, and then assumes they will spawn in the same manner.

Ever since aquariums became popular and inquisitive people became interested in the life habits of fishes, it has been tantalizing to make generalizations about fishes because of their eating, swimming, spawning and behavioral modes. Why is it, someone may ask, that most livebearers are top feeders with their mouths opening at the top? Why do most characins merely spray their eggs about in all directions and exhibit little if any parental care? Why do most fishes which require atmospheric air to supplement their ability of removing air from water

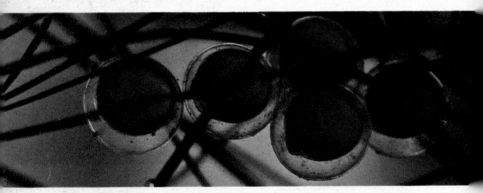

Typical appearance of developing fish eggs. These Red-bellied Piranha (Serrasalmus nattereri) eggs were produced by fish in captivity in Japan.

through gills have elaborate spawning rituals *(Betta, Corydoras)?* Is there any fish which makes a floating nest of bubbles *(Betta, Colisa, Trichogaster, Callichthys)* which is not an air-breather? Is there any Cichlid which, for one reason or another, doesn't mouth its eggs or young in one way or another? Why are livebearing fishes found only in coastal areas and not deep inland?

It is in the quest for the answer to some of these questions that thousands of people have taken fish-breeding as their hobby.

What I have tried to do here is gather all the general information I could properly illustrate about breeding aquarium fishes, and present it in such a way that it will lead aquarists into the rewarding position of having assisted in the creation of new life in this world. How many of us are lucky enough to be responsible for new life? It gives all fish breeders a wonderful feeling to look about in their breeding tanks and say to themselves, "If it weren't for my efforts, the life in these tanks wouldn't have existed."

HERBERT R. AXELROD

How To Breed Aquarium Fishes

One of the principal reasons for the rise in the number of people keeping and breeding aquarium fishes is that one can become an "expert" in a relatively short time. Every day a new fish appears in an aquarium store waiting for some ambitious hobbyist to discover its secrets. Usually the first person who breeds this fish becomes an authority on it as soon as his story is published in *Tropical Fish Hobbyist* magazine.

For those who want to report about fishes and how they spawn, it is necessary that their story contain certain essential facts. These facts are:

1. *What is the breeding season?* Do the fish breed all year long or only during certain seasons of the year?
2. *What diet were they fed to bring them into breeding condition?* Were they fed only freeze-dried foods, or did they have live foods or frozen foods as well? How often were they fed?
3. *What kind of water did they spawn in?* Such necessary items as pH, hardness, temperature, clarity and cleanliness are important.
4. *What breeding site did they select?* Did they spawn on a rock? Are they mouthbrooders? Did they spray eggs all about the aquarium?
5. *What are their secondary sex characteristics?* Assuming that primary sex characteristics are internal

A Splashing Tetra (Copella arnoldi) *breaking through the water's surface on its way to spawn on the leaf exposed above the water. Upon hatching the fry fall into the water below.*

organs (the gonads), how can you tell by looking at a living fish whether it is a male or female?

6. *What pre-spawning activity was noticed?* Did males fight between themselves? Were fish active before selecting a mate?

7. *What courtship rites did the pair go through prior to and during spawning?* Did one male mate with one female as with Cichlids? Or was mating a random thing as with most livebearers?

8. *How did actual mating take place?* Actual photographic representations of the spawning process are included in this book. Observe carefully and record impressions as they occur.

9. *What is the parental attitude toward the spawn after breeding?* Do the parents eat the eggs or do they protect them with their own lives?

10. *How long do the breeders live?* It is important that information be available as to how old the breeders were

A mouthbrooding fish, Pseudotropheus microstoma, *an African Cichlid in the act of collecting her fry; she is not eating them.*

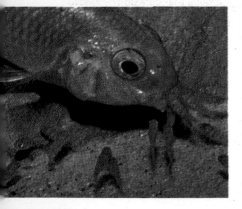

A Discus parent closely surrounded by a brood of grazing fry.

when they spawned. Of course for the first spawning of newly imported fish this is impossible. But after the first spawn it is relatively simple to consider when the tank-bred fish spawned. Most fishes spawn when they are half grown, but this is far from a hard-and-fast rule. If you breed a fish, determine how old the young are before they spawn. Then, if possible, determine how long the fish will live and during what period of their lives they breed.

11. *How do you feed and raise the fry?* For many years hobbyists had difficulty raising young Discus fish, *Symphysodon.* It was only after they learned that the fry must feed parasitically upon the parents that quantities of tank-bred discus became available.

If these questions, when answered, will lead to an accurate disclosure of how to breed an aquarium fish, then obviously the approach to breeding must follow the same path with educated guesses being made all along the way. Before this book deals with case histories of typical aquarium fishes, it should consider each of these ten areas in terms of the generalizations to be gained by the successful breeding of hundreds of different species and how those generalizations might apply to other, as yet unknown species.

The Breeding Season

A good deal of an aquarist's experience in breeding will be limited to the fishes of the order Cypriniformes. These cypriniform fishes are the second largest order (Perciformes being the

Knowing the living behavior of a fish in the wild is helpful. The African Cichlid Pseudotropheus lanisticola *requires a shell or its equivalent to exist and spawn in captivity.*

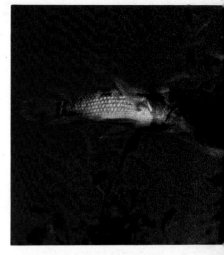

Knowing the eating habits of your fish is important. This Pike Cichlid (Crenicichla lepidota) *is a well known terror in the aquarium when in the company of other smaller species.*

largest), and are primarily freshwater fishes. The Cypriniformes usually is said to contain four distinct sub-orders of which two are of prime importance to the hobbyist. The four sub-orders are: the Catfishes (Siluroidei), the Electric Eels (Gymnotoidei), the Tetras or Characins (Characoidei) and the Loaches, Barbs and Minnows (Cyprinoidei). It is the last two groups that contain the species most often bred.

In nature, the same set of circumstances is rarely comparable to those in an aquarium at a given time. It is rare in nature that a male and female of the same species are completely isolated from predators and other members of the same species. The fact that it takes only a single male and a single female of the same species to spawn in an aquarium doesn't mean that only a single pair

13

spawns in nature. But because we know that only two fish *can spawn* we can assume that it is only *necessary* to have a pair. Some authors have found it much easier to have "community spawnings" than isolated pair spawnings. Examples of this can be found in the study of the Zebra Danio, *Brachydanio rerio* and other danios.

Thus when considering breeding season both natural and "civilized" problems have to be considered. In nature most, if not all, of the known aquarium fishes breed after the beginning of the rainy season when the rising water isolates the breeders from predatory fishes and when the increased fertilization of the waters brings forth a new chain of food from bacteria, protozoa and worms, to crustaceans and fry. Even annual fishes, which lay their eggs in the mud before the water dries out completely, must rely upon the rains to refill their pools so the eggs will hatch. The rains bring new mosquito generations and the new mosquitos lay eggs in the pools in which the developing annual fishes live, thus providing them with the food they need to thrive.

The "civilized" breeding season problems deal mostly with the available foods. Prior to the invention of freeze-dried brine shrimp and Tubifex worms, live foods were almost a necessity for most fishes if they were to be brought into breeding condition. Certainly Discus, Bettas, Angelfish and most Characins were not to be bred if live foods were not available. Now these problems are slowly disappearing and breeders are able, in many cases, to breed small fishes all year round.

In Florida, however, where most fishes are spawned to

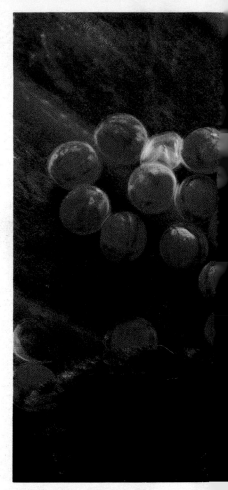

supply the aquarium market, the water is too cold to breed certain fishes outdoors during the winter months from November to April. Kissing Gouramis, Dwarf Gouramis, Oscars *(Astronotus ocellatus)* stop breeding after November, as do most all other egg-layers kept outdoors. Even the livebearing fishes such as the Swordtails and Platies *(Xiphophorus)*, Mollies and Guppies *(Poecilia)* fail to have many new young when the waters drop to 60° F in the outdoor pools. In aquariums, however, we successfully spawn fishes all year

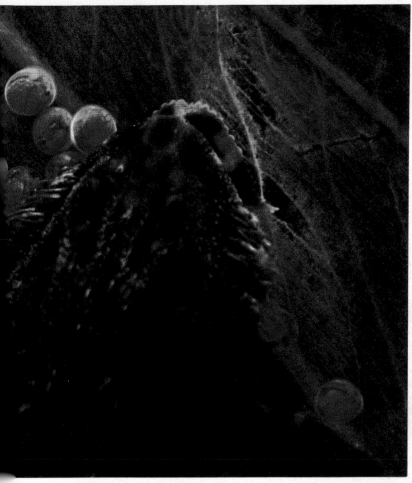

The eggs being guarded by this Loricariid Catfish (Rineloricaria) *are almost ready to hatch out. The embryos are almost fully formed.*

round, especially the livebearers, but the spring months of April and May are certainly the best months for all aquarium fishes, even those coming from the southern hemisphere originally.

So, for the hobbyist, his best chance is to attempt to spawn his new aquarium fish in the spring, though he might do well at other times of the year, too, providing proper foods are available. Oftentimes changes of water are recommended. It certainly can be generalized that most fishes prefer changes of 10 to 20 percent of their aquarium water every week (the water should be the same in terms of pH, DH and temperature) and perhaps these changes have the same effect that rain would have in their natural habitat. In commercial fish breeding where thousands of spawnings a week are recorded, it is always clean, fresh water that is used for breeding egg-layers. If the breeders don't spawn the first few days, they are replaced and the new breeders are set up in fresh water. Little success is experienced in breeding fishes in aged water which previously contained fishes.

Daphnia can be cultured at home or collected in natural ponds and waterways at certain seasons of the year.

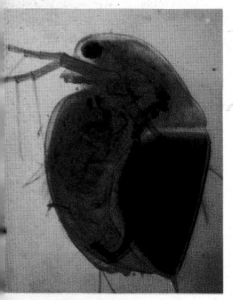

Maurice Rackowicz introduced frozen brine shrimp to the hobbyist. This was an ideal companion to the brine shrimp eggs produced in the Leslie Salt Flats south of San Francisco. The brine shrimp were ideal because they came from salt brine which almost sterilized the food from freshwater disease organisms. Breeders no longer had to worry about introducing harmful organisms into their aquariums when they fed the frozen or newly hatched brine shrimp. To this day, brine shrimp nauplii are still the ideal food for newly hatched fishes.

For a relatively low cost, you can have dry foods (flakes or freeze-dried) available to your fishes all year round. The dry foods come in a wide variety of substances. Liquid fry foods are also available today.

The Fishes' Diet

A fish's diet is important, not only to bring it into breeding condition, but to keep it alive and healthy. There is no question that for most fishes, live foods are best. But live foods have certain dangers. All too often, parasites and predators are introduced into an aquarium with the live foods. Diseases are very often initiated by an inoculation of live Daphnia, brine shrimp or Tubifex worms. So, what can the hobbyist do?

In the early days of the boom in fishkeeping, during the 1950's,

Brine Shrimp is a staple food for aquarium fish and easy to get.

Copepods are small crustaceans found in fresh and marine waters. They are part of the food chain in the natural habitat of fishes.

To feed your fishes properly, you should feed them as frequently as possible. To feed them frequently means that they should be fed as much as they can consume in five minutes, as often as possible. Even every hour if you can. It does not mean that you should throw in a handful of food so the fishes can eat as much and as often as they please. The food will decay, foul the tank and the resulting bacteria will kill the fishes.

An advantage of some freeze-dried foods is that they float and adhere to the glass wall of the aquarium when pressed against it. Thus, by sticking a chunk of worms onto the glass (or feeding the worms or brine shrimp in a feeding bell) you can constantly observe exactly how fast the food is being consumed and can

ascertain when more food should be offered. The usual prepared foods fall to the bottom where they might fall into crevices in the gravel and foul before they are eaten.

In any case, a female should start to round out as she comes into condition, and a male should become more colorful. These are the results of proper feeding regardless of what or how you fed.

Live Tubifex worms are sold in pet shops at reasonable cost. They can survive for a few days under refrigeration in the home.

How to Breed Aquarium Fishes

Your local pet dealer can recommend the type of filter that is appropriate for the capacity of your fish tank.

when kept in captivity. It is important that the fish breeder have some idea of aquarium water chemistry and consult different books on the subject if water is his problem.

Water has many, many characteristics. It can contain almost every known gas, every soluble salt, have different colors, and have a temperature range from 33° F., just above freezing, to 211° F., just below boiling. It can range from acid to alkaline, depending upon the material dissolved in it. Or it can contain a poison, such as DDT, which in strength will kill fishes almost instantly.

The Water

The life and death of most fishes in captivity is dependent more upon the aquarium water than any other single characteristic. Many die from overfeeding (not over*eating*). But more fishes die from water shock or poisoning than from any other single cause

A power head when in operation on the undergravel filter provides aeration which can be reduced or increased to suit the requirements of your project.

Unsightly algae growing on the glass walls of a tank can be removed with a scraper. The loose debris floats into the water and is removed by the filtering system.

Every successful fish breeder knows the characteristics of his water supply intimately. He knows if the local water supply company has changed its source of water, or has added more chlorine to the water. He knows it because he sees the way fishes react when they are put into this "new" water.

It is not within the scope of this book to probe into the characteristics of water and to explain water chemistry. It is only our attempt to highlight as simply as possible what it is that makes

Every aquarist should have a pH kit. It is easy to use and not too costly.

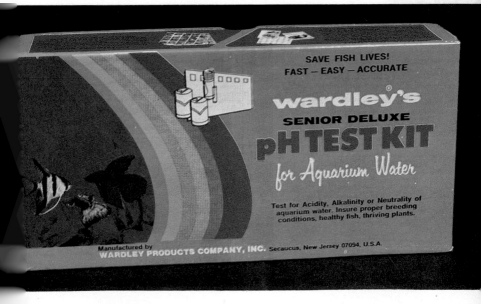

SAVE FISH LIVES!
FAST — EASY — ACCURATE

wardley's
SENIOR DELUXE
pH TEST KIT
for Aquarium Water

Test for Acidity, Alkalinity or Neutrality of aquarium water. Insure proper breeding conditions, healthy fish, thriving plants.

Manufactured by
WARDLEY PRODUCTS COMPANY, INC. Secaucus, New Jersey 07094, U.S.A.

fishes spawn in one kind of water and perish in another.

To generalize, most fishes will do well in neutral, soft water. This is water wih a pH of about 7.0. Many fishes, especially the egg-scatterers, spawn more readily in acid water, water with a pH of 6.4 to 6.8. Most livebearers, on the other hand, as well as many Cichlids, seem to prefer slightly alkaline water with a pH in the neighborhood of 7.6. There are some African cichlids that like their water decidedly hard and alkaline—even a pH of over 8 being enjoyed.

a pH range of 6.4 to 7.0, a water temperature of 72° to 80° F. and as soft as possible, without relying at all on distilled or rain water.

Central American fishes seem to prefer harder, more alkaline water, especially the Cichlids and livebearers. They should have water with a pH of 7.0 to 7.8, and harder than usual. If your tap water is soft, add a small amount of non-iodized salt.

Asian fishes have the same requirements as the South American fishes, while Australian fishes have the same general

Although Guppies (Poecilia reticulata) *often prefer brackish water in nature, they have adapted to thrive in almost any freshwater situation.*

When you have an unknown fish on your hands, it is best to maintain it in water in which you "guess" it will do best. This "guess" will be determined by the closest relative of the fish that you have experience with. If the fish is an annual fish from Africa or South America, try to maintain it in water in which you had success with other fishes of the same group. If you are starting with a fish you know nothing at all about, try to find someone who can tentatively identify the fish for you. Generally speaking, all South American fishes do best in neutral to slightly acid water with

requirements as the Central American fishes. African fishes can be categorized by their habitat. The lake fishes require relatively hard, alkaline water while the stream fishes require soft, acid water.

Petshops have inexpensive pH kits, water hardness kits, and thermometers. You can't breed or maintain fishes without their use.

Another characteristic of water is its color. Many German hobbyists claim success only with the use of peat moss which makes the water acid and dark brown at the same time. However more fishes are bred in Florida and Hong Kong than in all of Germany and the rest of Europe combined, and nowhere in Florida or Hong Kong did the author ever see the use of peat moss. Perhaps for the water in Germany peat moss is good. For the hard, alkaline waters of Palmetto, Florida, where the smell of sulphur is so strong as the water comes out of the ground, peat moss is worthless.

Fishes do seem to be happier in water which is stained a light tan from peat moss, and water which has peat moss in it does have a lower bacterial count. However, one can depend on a strong filter that can keep the water in good condition.

Breeding Sites

Many Dwarf Cichlids spawn in the secrecy of a flowerpot. Many Tetras spawn in the open waters, spraying their eggs haphazardly on vegetation. Will Dwarf Cichlids spawn on vegetation if there are no rocks or flowerpot available? Will Tetras spawn in a flowerpot if no vegetation is available?

The answer to both questions is "No." Cichlids must have a proper place upon which to deposit their spawn. They almost always prepare this site with an intense devotion to sanitation. They cleanse it thoroughly with their mouths. They ascertain privacy and relative protection from predators. They uproot all plants which are close to the spawning site so other fishes which might eat their eggs or young cannot hide from their view. It seems that without these necessary items, a Cichlid cannot achieve the correct "psychological" attitude and will not begin his spawning drive.

The same is true of certain Characins. If they are kept in a

A clay flowerpot is certain to be chosen as a spawning site by most Dwarf Cichlids. This male Apistogramma ortmanni *is guarding a clutch of eggs.*

Fine-leafed plants or any artificial equivalent is indispensable for spawning fish that spray eggs at random, like the Glowlight Tetra (Hemigrammus erythrozonus), *shown here.*

bare tank with no vegetation at all, chances are they will not spawn, though the female will certainly ripen as this is the way they are ripened in most commercial hatcheries.

It seems necessary to generalize the spawning site requirements of fishes as follows:

CICHLIDS—no plants, large flat rocks, flowerpots inverted on their sides and large enough to comfortably accommodate an adult pair of fishes. Gravel on the bottom of the tank.

CHARACINS—thickly planted on one end or corner with bushy plants or thickets. No gravel on the tank bottom. No rocks or flowerpots.

BARBS—same as Characins.

LIVEBEARERS—thickly planted all over so babies are hidden from parents. Floating plants are also recommended so the newborn can hide among the floating leaves and roots.

Needless to say, the larger the fish, the larger must be the aquarium in which the fishes will

Suggested plant arrangement for a community or display tank. For greatest success in breeding fish, use a setup that simulates the natural habitat of the species.

spawn. For a pair of Cardinal Tetras, each one inch long, an aquarium from two to five gallons is large enough.

For breeding Characins, a glass bottom tank is almost a necessity. The tank should be covered all over the bottom or a good part of it with bushy plants or Spanish moss spawning grass. Plastic spawning grasses also can be used. To ascertain whether the fishes have spawned shine a light through the bottom as you view it from the top. This bottom lighting highlights the eggs.

Of course, with Cichlids, a large piece of slate or a flat rock is necessary as the fishes spawn on it. For mouthbrooders, most dig a depression in the sand where the eggs are deposited and fertilized before one of them begins the

The spawning ritual of most fishes includes the meticulous cleaning of the nesting site. Providing them with a smooth piece of rock will help encourage breeding. Shown is Aequidens dorsigerus, *a South American Cichlid.*

mirror effect which reflects light. Painting the bottom black on the outside or pasting a piece of dark paper can solve this problem.Cleanliness is easier to achieve without gravel. Wherever possible, eliminate gravel from the breeding aquarium.

period of oral incubation. Livebearers, of course, are usually unconcerned about their aquarium bottom as long as no light comes from the bottom. They are usually surface breeders and spend most of their time near the top of the aquarium. For this reason they are quite uncomfortable when any light comes from the bottom. Glass bottom tanks which have no gravel on the bottom often have a

The presence of some thickets of plants where the eggs fall through reduces the predation on the eggs by the parents. Dwarf Pencilfish (Nannostomus marginatus), *seen here, actively look for their own eggs as food after spawning.*

Secondary Sex Characteristics

The primary sex characteristics are the gonads, that is, the ovaries and testes. Any other differences between males and females of fishes of the same species are to be considered as secondary sex characteristics. Generally speaking, a fish is born either a male or female and with nearly all fishes, the young fish can only be sexually differentiated by dissection. Therefore, for aquarists' purposes, we can define the secondary sexual characteristics as any *external* characteristic which may be observed without recourse to dissection.

With all livebearers, for example, one of the most obvious of the secondary sex characteristics is the intromittent organ or gonopodium. This is the thickened, fused anal fin of the male. The female has a normal anal fin, as do young fish of both sexes. As a typical livebearer matures, the males' anal fin begins to fuse and thicken, becoming the familiar gonopodium which is movable

The presence of egg spots on the anal fin is characteristic of the male Nigerian Mouthbrooder (Haplochromis burtoni). *These spots are often called "egg dummies."*

and used for the internal fertilization of the female. In some cases the gonopodium is actually inserted into the female. In other cases it merely directs the sperm packet (spermatophore) to the general vicinity of the genital pore of the female.

The sperm packet of most livebearers is shaped like a typical hen's egg, but much smaller of course. Within minutes after the spermatophores are introduced into the genital tract of the female livebearer, the individual sperm are released from the packets. Most female livebearers are able to actually store the sperm for future use and one mating may suffice for the fertilization of many generations. Thus many aquarists succumb to fantastic tales of hybridizing between Mollies and Swordtails, for example.

As an example most referred to

by letters received from beginning fish breeders, let's take a look at the Guppy. The males are usually much more colorful than the females. They also have longer fins, especially their unpaired fins, and the males have a gonopodium. The females are always larger in body size than the males of the same strain. All of these characteristics (finnage, color, body size, gonopodium) are secondary sex characteristics. The male inserts his gonopodium into the genital pore of the female and shoots a sperm packet into the female. Almost immediately the sperm packet dissolves and the sperms wiggle their way up the oviduct to a storage area from which they eventually find their way back to the ovary where the ripening eggs are to be found. If there is another mating with another male, some of his sperm might be expected to be mingled with the sperm of previous matings, so future broods of the particular female might have one, two, or a score of different fathers.

Such terms as "viviparous" and "ovoviviparous" have been applied to most livebearing fishes at one time or another in the literature. A *viviparous* fish is one that contributes some nourishment to the young it carries. The egg is internally fertilized and develops fully, the young being born alive and self-sufficient. An *ovoviviparous* fish is one that contributes only the egg to the new fry. The egg is internally fertilized and it usually stays inside the female (there are exceptions) until it is hatched, at which time it is expelled from the female. The author has taken thousands of fertilized, developing eggs from female livebearers, only to have them die in a relatively short time. This would indicate that the developing embryos do receive nourishment from their mothers.

The egglayers have completely different secondary sex characteristics. With the Cichlid

The sword (an elongated ray of the caudal fin) is developed only in the male Swordtail (Xiphophorus helleri) *which also possesses a copulatory organ, the gonopodium.*

group, the mature fishes are almost always distinguishable from each other by color (the male's is usually more intense), length of fins (the male has longer, more pointed anal and dorsal fins), and, in such cases as Angelfish *(Pterophyllum)* and Discus *(Symphysodon)* by the bulging sides of a female swollen with roe. With young Cichlids it is

The male Siamese Fighting Fish (Betta splendens) *develops long, flowing fins while the female has fins of normal length. Males are definitely more colorful and pugnacious than females.*

almost impossible to tell.

These same characteristics are true of most of the Anabantids such as the Paradise fish *(Macropodus)* and the Fighting Fish *(Betta)*. In the Siamese Fighting Fish, the great difference in size between the male's finnage and the female's is quite exaggerated since breeders have been selectively breeding for longer fins and more colorful bodies in the males. But in wild fish there is not that much difference in coloration and finnage size. These elongated fins, especially dorsals and anals, can be found not only in Cichlids and Anabantids, but also in some Barbs and some livebearers.

In many cases there are no obvious secondary sex characteristics. But even with these exceptional species, like the Angelfish, the female when ready to spawn nearly always has her ovipositor (a small white nipple projecting from her anal pore) in

External differences between the sexes are not perceptible in many fishes. This fancy variety of Angelfish (Pterophyllum scalare) *can not be sexed except much later when ready to breed. The female's abdomen becomes enlarged with roe and her ovipositor protrudes.*

position before the male shows his breeding tube. Furthermore, hers is thicker than the male's. It is part of the aquarist's task to ascertain the sex characteristics of his fishes and a spawning report which doesn't contain information on sexing is incomplete.

How to Breed Aquarium Fishes

Two Blue Acaras (Aequidens pulcher) *engaged in jaw-locking display. If the pair is compatible neither fish will be seriously injured.*

Pre-Spawning Activity

The most interesting aspect of fish breeding, aside from financial reward, is the observation of the pair in their courting and nest preparation. The photographs which accompany most of this text serve to highlight in detail the elaborate steps a pair of fishes will take in site selection, site preparation, nest preparation, spawning, fighting and fry care.

The most significant pre-spawning activity is mate selection for those fishes which spawn in pairs. In the aquarium, the breeder does the selection for the most part. He looks for a female showing all the characteristics of color, vigor, health, robustness, ripeness and size. She should be moderately full of eggs and she should have been conditioned on live foods for a few weeks prior to spawning.

The male should have the same general characteristics. He should be very active, extremely colorful, vigorous and be about the same size as the female if possible.

In most cases the female should be introduced to the breeding tank a day before the male is introduced. If the female is larger than the male they can both be introduced at the same time. Initially the pair will usually ignore each other. This is especially true of most Anabantids (Bettas and Gouramis), Danios, Characins, Barbs and livebearers. But in a short time they begin to flirt. In Siamese Fighting Fish, we know the male will tear up the female a bit before he gets down to the job of building his bubblenest. Some of the Barbs will chew up the anal fins of females who are unwilling or unable to spawn. Livebearers and most Characins will ignore a

A male Cichlid, also of the genus Aequidens, *is shown here removing a fairly big piece of stone from a possible nesting site.*

Note the damaged fins of this female Betta. Upon completion of spawning, she is usually removed, and the care of the bubble nest is left to the male.

mate who is unable or unwilling to breed. But Cichlids are for the most part very different. For the time being we shall ignore Angelfish and Discus, for they are much more timid than the usual Cichlids and the pairs can and should stay together for as long as they live. For the other Cichlids, care should be taken that both are of equal size and strength for it not unusual for one of them to kill the other in battles of strength.

It is usual for mating Cichlids to lock jaws and spar about the tank. Most breeders agree that if this jaw-locking ceremony is successful, the pair will begin the next step in the spawning ritual. No one knows what "successful" is when it comes to jaw-locking, so be prepared to remove one or the other if the fighting gets too rough and one of them hides from the other without fighting back. In

Floating plants aid in keeping the bubblenest together. Note the egg of this Betta on the verge of being dropped.

most cases it only means that the time was not ripe for the female and another week or two of conditioning will do it.

Pre-spawning activity for Characins is finding a bunch of plants. For Cichlids it is clearing a site for spawning with a large flat rock or in a cave they have dug. For Anabantids it is building a bubblenest.

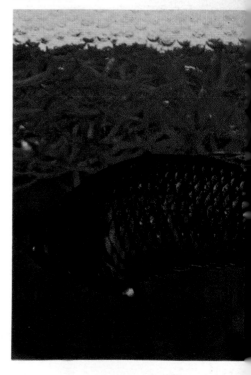

Courtship Rituals

In the previous section which dealt with pre-spawning activity, there had to be a fine line drawn between actual pre-spawning activity (such as locking jaws) and courtship rituals which might include a male *Betta* dancing in front of a female with outstretched fins, seducing her under his nest of bubbles much like a bullfighter tantalizes a bull with a red cape. What really interests us here is something different. If you place a male Cichlid with a dozen females of the same species, he will select

The red marking of Bloodfins, as these Characoids are known, becomes intense among the males during breeding. The females have a reddish tinge, but never as bright.

These are the males of two different Killifish (Nothobranchius) species, very similar in many aspects except coloration. Females are not as colorful.

only one with which to breed. If you put a male *Aphyosemion* or *Brachydanio* with a dozen females he will try to breed with them all. The same is true of many Characins, Barbs, *Corydoras, Rasbora, Tanichthys* and all livebearers. Many breeders have gone through the experimental stages of multiple pairs in a spawning tank and nearly all have decided they get more eggs if they isolate pairs, or at most, use a trio. With Cichlids, a pair is always best except when trying to find pairs. All commercial breeders raise a group of

Angelfish together and isolate the pairs as they mate. The same is true of many Dwarf Cichlids, mainly because it is almost impossible in many cases to know which female of a species goes with which male.

Observe how your fishes paired off and what characteristics of courtship they exhibited so you can have an idea of how to approach a new fish when attempting to breed it.

During courtship and spawning only the male Nothobranchius *develops the most brilliant coloration; the females remain inconspicuous throughout life.*

Except for the size of the female's abdomen, this pair of Head-and-Tail Light Tetras (Hemigrammus ocellifer) *exhibit the same color pattern and brightness.*

A typical spawning embrace exhibited by many bubblenest builders. The male Honey Gourami (Colisa chuna) wraps his body around the female, as both eggs and sperm are released.

The Pearl Danio (Brachydanio albolineatus) *breeds with ease in captivity. It can be placed in the category of a beginner's fish.*

Actual Mating

Less is known about actual fertilization than most breeders realize. Even though millions of breeders have watched Swordtails, Platies, Mollies and Guppies copulate, no one is certain whether or not, *at that particular moment,* the male effected penetration of the female. In most cases, the momentary contacts that Guppies are so famous for result in no contact and no fertilization at all. A much longer contact, easily observed in most Mollies, is what is usually required for fertilization.

Corydoras species, where the female goes through such an elaborate ritual with males wherein she mouths the male's genital pore prior to depositing her eggs, has led many to believe that she takes sperm into her mouth, swallows it and thus fertilizes her own eggs internally. This is, of course, impossible. The author has dissected about a dozen female *Corydoras aeneus* which were alive and immediately thrust into ice water during the height of their spawning ritual, and in no case did he find sperm either in the mouth or any place in the digestive tract.

In all probability she takes the sperm into her mouth immediately prior to depositing her eggs in position on the aquarium glass, a rock, or some suitable plant leaf.

Siamese Fighting Fish, of course, fertilize their eggs during their nuptial embrace where the male squeezes the eggs from the female and fertilizes them as they are released. Since he catches many of the eggs in his mouth prior to depositing them into his bubblenest, many breeders suggested that he, too, fertilized them in his mouth. But it is possible to take some of the eggs from the spawning before the male has a chance to mouth them. They can easily be seen to be fertilized and developing under a very low power microscope.

Non-mouthbrooding Cichlids generally spawn with the female laying her eggs on a prepared site. The eggs are adhesive. The general pattern is that the male fertilizes them after the female has laid a string of them. They take turns. The female deposits ten or so eggs, and the male

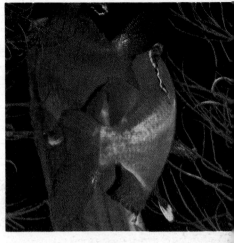

Prior to actual spawning the partners proceed to lie side by side, as viewed from the rear in this pair of Tetras of the genus Hyphessobrycon.

The eggs of Killifishes are deliberately trapped in the spawning grass and are collected by hand later. Being annual fish, this pair of Nothobranchius rachovi will not survive many months after starting to spawn. Few annuals survive two years even in an aquarium.

This Gourami (Colisa) couple is partially immobilized at the bottom of the tank after a spawning embrace; note the released eggs.

Certain species of fish can develop a characteristic hump on the forehead that becomes more prominent with advancing age. These are young Lionhead Cichlids (Steatocranus casuarius).

comes along and fertilizes them. This is kept up until sometimes thousands of eggs are deposited and the entire rock or other spawning site is completely covered with eggs.

With Characins, Barbs and Danios, fertilization takes place as the pair push against each other in the plant thickets. In many cases the male uses his dorsal fin to hold the female against him while their S-curve against each other forces the eggs from the female and the sperm from the male. Artificial "milking" of both male and female is simple if the pair are interrupted during spawning.

Longevity

How long a fish lives and what is the length of time during which it can breed seem to be the same question. Fishes, unlike mammals, seem to keep growing every year even though their rate of growth slows down. Obviously a fish or almost any other animal grows fastest immediately after it is born. But if we take the average age of a livebearer to be two years old when it dies of "old age," we would have to consider that 90 percent of its growth takes place during the first six months of its life.

There are no accurate records published on how long fishes live, though many public aquariums have such data available for isolated animals and fishes. The scales of fishes give a clue as to their age, but with the small aquarium fishes no one has bothered to study them. If you spawn fishes, keep accurate records of the spawning date and how long the fishes live, how old they were when they first bred and how old they were when they stopped breeding.

Frozen Brine Shrimp, from newly hatched to full-size adults, are marketed in convenient packets that can easily be stored in the home freezer.

Your local pet shop dealer, more often than not, offers live Brine Shrimp of all stages of development. He also probably sells Brine Shrimp eggs that you can hatch yourself.

Feeding The Fry

When the beginner breeds his first fish, chances are he will lose most or all of them during the first week of their life. The main reason is that he is not prepared to receive them and has no food ready to feed them. Without exception all fish just born do not need food until they are free-swimming. With those fishes, like most of the livebearers, which are born free-swimming, they need food almost immediately. The egglaying fishes have enough nourishment in the egg that the newborn fishes don't require feeding until the fry are swimming.

There is no better food than nature's own infusoria for newly hatched fishes. In the old days of the hobby, breeders would cultivate microscopic cultures and identify some of the protozoans (they still argue which is the best food, *Paramecium* or *Euglena*), maintaining pure cultures to feed their developing fry. In rare cases would they raise more than 50 percent of the eggs they had. Today things are more convenient. With the availability of brine shrimp eggs newborn Cichlids, livebearers and some larger Characins, can take newly-hatched brine shrimp immediately. Fortunately there are many kinds of brine shrimp. The brine shrimp from the Great Salt Lake in Utah are not suitable to feed most of the small newborn fry. They are too large. In San Francisco (the Leslie Salt Flats) a smaller egg is available and the newly-hatched nauplii of the San Francisco brine shrimp are ideal for even the smallest mouth. A week or so on newly-hatched brine shrimp and the fry are old enough to be fed the Utah brine shrimp.

The whole idea is to have food

in front of the fry at all times as they are continuously hungry. One day without food and nearly all will perish. After the first week, most of the danger is gone. The second and third weeks find the fry growing well but still requiring plenty of food. The whole problem with raising the youngsters is to feed them well at all times, but to keep the tank from fouling. This is where experience comes in.

If the water gets cloudy, stop feeding for a few days for the cloudy water usually contains enough micro-organisms to sufficiently feed the fish for a day or two.

If you learn how to feed your baby fishes, you have most of the job learned. The two most difficult jobs of the commercial breeder are selecting the best fish to put together to spawn, and feeding the fry. Feeding the fry is by far the most difficult.

The following case histories of typical aquarium fishes represent the important breeding types found among many egglaying fishes and that of a livebearing fish, the Guppy. They are loosely arranged according to the systematic classification of the fish.

CICHLIDS—Angelfish; Convict Cichlid; Firemouth Cichlid; Jack Dempsey; Oscar; Discus.

DWARF CICHLIDS—Blunthead Cichlid; Kribensis; Egyptian Mouthbrooder.

CHARACOIDS—Dwarf Pencilfish; Neon Tetra; Red-bellied Piranha.

CYPRINIDS—Tiger Barb; Rosy Barb; Zebra Danio; Harlequin; White Cloud.

CATFISHES—Bronze Catfish.

KILLIFISHES—Striped Panchax; Lyretail; Günther's Notho; White's Cynolebias.

ANABANTOIDS—Siamese Fighting Fish; Dwarf Gourami; Paradise Fish; Three-spot or Blue Gourami.

POECILIIDS—Guppy.

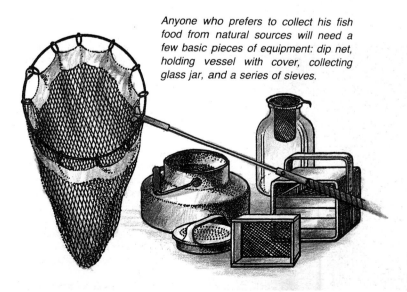

Anyone who prefers to collect his fish food from natural sources will need a few basic pieces of equipment: dip net, holding vessel with cover, collecting glass jar, and a series of sieves.

The Angelfish

Pterophyllum scalare

The famous Angelfish has been known to aquarium hobbyists for quite a time. The first specimens to be brought in were considered to be one of the "problem fishes" because it was very difficult to get a pair to mate and spawn. After tank-raised stock became available even novices could breed them.

As with other Cichlid species, the person who desires to have them spawn for him has to make a decision whether to let the eggs hatch naturally with the parents watching over them or to "play it safe" and hatch the eggs artificially by agitating the water over them with an airstone.

A larger-sized aquarium is advisable for breeding this species, at least 20 gallons. The best temperature is about 78° F. The water should be neutral to slightly acid. It is better to dispense with plants or gravel on the bottom, and it has been found that the best foundation for the eggs is a strip of slate about 2 inches wide, resting at an angle against the side of the aquarium. If you have a number of Angelfish to work with let nature take its course and use a pair that has "chosen" each other. This is not an act of intelligence, but it is a means of getting together a pair where the male and the female are ripe.

The pair will begin by becoming greatly interested in the strip of slate. They go over it and meticulously clean off any bit of algae or dirt they find. Finally the female swims over the slate, her

Cleaning the spawning site, in this case a flat leaf, is normal behavior for Angelfish spawning and is typical of any substrate-spawning Cichlid before spawning.

A pair of Marble Angelfish guarding and fanning the egg clutch.

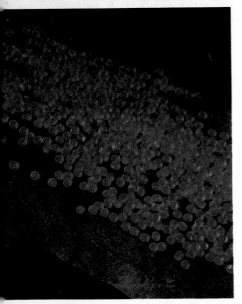

belly almost touching it and leaving behind a string of eggs. The male swims close behind, spraying the eggs with his sperm. String after string of eggs is stuck to the surface of the slate by the female and dutifully fertilized by the male. When the spawning process is finished, the pair will go over their work, circulating water over the eggs by waving their fins, and "mouthing" them individually. Many writers give the fish in this group credit for the intelligence of being able to spot

Appearance of a healthy clutch of eggs.

infertile eggs and picking them out and eating them. This is not the case at all. When a bad egg is taken into the fish's mouth it bursts, and the egg is not eaten but expelled through the gills.

Hatching takes place in one or two days, and in four or five days more the little ones have absorbed their yolk-sacs and begun an active search for food. For the first week, they can be fed with the time-honored system of squeezing some hard-boiled egg yolk through a piece of cloth. Then they can be fed newly-hatched brine shrimp.

The prime disadvantage of leaving the breeders with the fry is they sometimes proceed to eat the entire batch of eggs or young. The alternate system, of course, eliminates the need for having the parents there. The eggs are taken into another aquarium after the parents have finished laying and fertilizing them. There a stream of air-bubbles is allowed to rise near the eggs, causing the water to become slightly agitated. The eggs which have turned white may be removed with an ordinary eye-dropper, and the youngsters cared for in the usual manner. This is the system used by commercial breeders to turn out huge quantities of Angelfish as well as most of the other Cichlid species. It deprives the hobbyist of the pleasure of seeing the youngsters watched over tenderly by the parents, but it is the safer method of getting the youngsters raised.

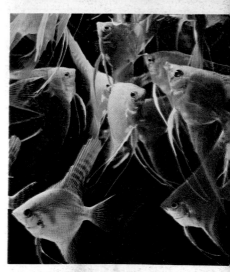

Angelfish fry of the Golden variety in various stages of development: (Top) *about four weeks old.* (Center) *six weeks old.* (Bottom) *well past the six-week point.*

The Convict Cichlid

Cichlasoma nigrofasciatum

The Zebra or Convict Cichlids from Central America are predaceous and cannot be trusted with smaller fishes.

Their color is very variable. Some have yellow backs with a purple sheen along the sides, and a pale gray belly. Others are a plain silver with characteristic vertical bands. Usually they have bluish or pearly gray sides with eight to nine black transverse bars. As the fish ages these bars decrease in number. The fins are a fine metallic green. Members of this species are quite high strung and change color rapidly when excited or frightened.

C. nigrofasciatum grow to six inches; they begin breeding at half this size. They eat almost anything they are fed.

Breeding these fish is extremely easy if they are given just the barest essentials. They spawn in the typical Cichlid fashion. The breeding tank should be about 15 to 20 gallons with a 2-inch sand bottom. They will uproot and chew plants prior to breeding so the tank should be bare except for a few large flat rocks, pieces of slate arranged in arches or an inverted flower pot. The water conditions are not critical. The temperature may range from 68° to 80°F., the optimum for breeding however is 75°F. Water should be moderately hard, with a pH of about 7.2.

The pair should be placed in this tank by themselves and conditioned on copious feedings of brine shrimp and Tubifex worms. The females are the aggressors and the more colorful. The transverse bars become a deep brick red during the breeding season. This greater color in the females is extraordinary among Cichlids. The males are usually smaller and their bands fade during the

The Convict Cichlid will clean the spawning site without fail before spawning occurs.

Unless the eggs are aerated by fanning with the pectorals and mouthed to remove debris, they will die and become fungused.

breeding season and are replaced by gleaming metallic areas.

Spawning will readily take place if they are in good condition. They take extremely good care of their brood. They herd the fry into pre-dug hollows in the sand when they are free swimming. The females are often scrappy at this time so the male should be removed after breeding. The spawns are large. The young are attractively striped. They thrive on fry food, brine shrimp, and Infusoria the first week after hatching.

The female assumes most of the responsibility for the care of the spawn, but the male often plays a large part.

A successful breeding of Convict Cichlids produces very many fry, but not all are expected to reach adulthood.

The Firemouth Cichlid

Cichlasoma meeki

The Firemouths are beautiful, popular fish. They are rather peaceful for Cichlids but cannot be kept with smaller fishes. They are carnivorous and should be given a varied diet of predominately living food. They can become quite tame and learn to take food from your fingers. If fed a proper diet the male will reach a size of 5 inches; the female is 1 inch smaller. When in top condition they will breed at 2 inches. The water conditions are not critical; the temperature may range from 68° to 85°F. It is necessary to keep them in a large tank, 15 gallons or greater, with some open areas and a number of rock formations for shelter. The water should be slightly alkaline (7.2 pH).

C. meeki are native to northern Yucatan. They have quite flashy coloration. Their body is a bluish gray, with a violet sheen; their back is darker. There are a number of vertical bars and a horizontal stripe runs across the body. The unpaired fins are edged with blue-green; the other fins are a yellowish to reddish brown. A fiery orange covers the belly and sometimes runs up into the throat and mouth.

Members of this species make good parents and well mated pairs will spawn readily. Prior to spawning, colors deepen, a bright red flush extends over the belly and chin and up into the mouth of the male. When fully mature, he will develop a long filament at the

Two Firemouths confront each other to see who will eventually breed with the female.

tip of his dorsal. Until the fish are mature it is rather difficult to distinguish the two sexes. The female's colors are more subdued; her fins are shorter and her body fuller.

At spawning time the male becomes quite impatient and may kill the female if she is not ready.

The protrusible mouth seen in this female Firemouth enables her to clean the spawning site and to gather the fry later.

The breeding tank should be large with a number of natural rock formations. The breeders don't tolerate plant life and plants are torn and sand dug up prior to spawning. A corner will be staked out. It is best to allow the male to choose his own mate. The two will grip each other by the mouth in a tug of war. If this ends in a stalemate, the chances are good the pair will get along well. The

The red coloration of the male Firemouth is truly impressive. The less colorful female is busy depositing eggs in the cave.

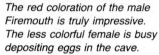

spawning site will be meticulously cleaned. Afterwards the male will swim in steadily decreasing circles around his mate. The eggs are laid on a prepared site and carefully fanned for two to three days until they hatch. The spawnings are large and the young are easily raised. After birth the fry are transported in their parents' mouths to a number of shallow depressions or pits. They are moved around from hole to hole at frequent intervals. If kept at 78°F., they will become free-swimming after three or four days. They are a good size and can eat quite large amounts of freshly hatched brine shrimp. The parents are best removed at this time.

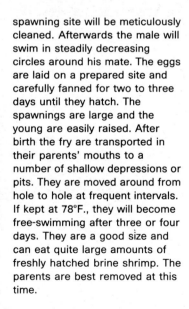

Viewed frontally, the extensive throat pouch of the male Firemouth is evident. The young fry, presumably attracted to the red color, will stay close to the guarding male parent.

The Jack Dempsey

Cichlasoma octofasciatum
The Jack Dempsey Cichlids, from the Rio Negro, the Amazon Basin and Costa Rica, are very aggressive, as their common name indicates. They love to dig and uproot plants and should be kept only with larger fish which can take care of themselves.

They are quite handsome; otherwise they would be avoided because of their pugnacious disposition. Their brilliant coloration, unlike many Cichlids, is not likely to change under emotional excitement or fear. Their body is brown to black with a dark spot in the center and another at the base of the tail. They are peppered with brilliant light blue spots all over their body and fins. The female shows only a few of these. The male has a bright red edge on his dorsal and anal fins, both of which are longer and more pointed than those of his mate. These colors become more fixed with age.

Having such a blue iridescent coloration, Jack Dempseys are popular, in spite of their aggressive nature that some aquarists find also desirable.

Jack Dempseys are typical Cichlids and jaw-locking before breeding is a normal aspect of their breeding behavior.

The male grows to a length of about 8 inches; the female is slightly smaller. They will usually breed at 5 inches. They have quite a hearty appetite.

Being large and tough they need a large unplanted tank. They are hardy and will often live to 10 years or more. If well conditioned they will spawn readily. They breed in the typical Cichlid manner. They require a fairly

Hundreds of eggs are produced during breeding.

A nutritious type of food must be provided for breeders of any kind of fish.

large breeding tank filled with normal tap water and stocked with floating plants. The temperature should be raised gradually to 78° F. Spawning will take place on a flat rock or flower pot. Prior to spawning breeding tubes will be noticeable in the region of the vent. As is common among the Cichlids, they make fond and gentle parents, taking excellent care of eggs and fry. They are egg anchorers. While spawning their color intensifies to a brilliant deep blue.

Well known for their aggressiveness toward other fishes, Jack Dempseys take care of the brood seriously.

The Oscar

Astronotus ocellatus

The Oscar, as he is affectionately called by many, has been adopted by a great many people who bought a couple of cute youngsters without the slightest inkling of how big they would get. Unlike the case with many other Cichlid owners whose fish also grow to a respectable size, an Oscar owner would never think of getting rid of his pets, mainly because they seem to have a winning personality all their own. They are very quick to recognize the person who feeds them, and some specimens even act affectionately toward their owners, coming to the surface to get their backs scratched and nibbling at a finger offered to them.

Keeping a full-sized pair of Oscars calls for a rather large tank, at least 50 gallons in capacity. Sexes are not quite as easy to distinguish as with many other Cichlids. The male has slightly larger fins and more and larger red areas on his sides. The only sure way is to compare the breeding tubes when they are ready to spawn. The female's tube is wider and more blunt, and the male's is narrower and more pointed. Oscars are not particularly choosy about the water in which they are kept, as long as it is reasonably clean. For breeding, it is best to give them optimum conditions of about pH 7.5 and a DH of about 10 to 15. The temperature should be 76° to 80° F. There should be several

These Oscars are quite large and if expected to breed successfully the selected breeders must be placed in a very large tank.

Both male and female Oscar share in guarding the eggs.

even feed them small lumps of canned dog foods, but here overfeeding is a risk that must be avoided.

Oscar courtship varies greatly: in some cases the pair gets along very amicably and in many the male, and sometimes even the female, gets rough. If injuries are seen to result, separate the pair until the injured one recovers.

It is difficult to predict where a pair will spawn. Generally a smooth rock will get the preference. Sometimes they will dig down through several inches of gravel to get to the smooth bottom and deposit their eggs there. Large spawnings, 500 eggs or more, are not infrequent. The female goes over the chosen surface, rubbing her belly against it. When after a few false starts her eggs finally appear in a row behind her, the male follows close behind, fertilizing them as they appear.

While all this is going on the pair should be disturbed as little as possible. Stay away from the tank and if you must watch make few sudden moves. The breeders are very nervous and high-strung at this time and any movement that they can see might be misconstrued as an attempt to get at the precious eggs. Some Cichlid breeders cover the front of the breeding tank with heavy paper that has a small hole cut in it. Observation is done through this hole, usually without the breeding pair's knowledge that there is anything going on. This paper is best left on until the fry are free-swimming and the parents are removed. This system can be used successfully for many of the larger Cichlid species. Unless you are anxious to see the parents care for their young and are willing to gamble on their being eaten, this is the time to

large rocks placed at their disposal, not only to hold the eggs but to give the female, or perchance the male, an opportunity to hide if necessary. Putting plants in an Oscar tank is usually a waste of time; they generally get uprooted.

Needless to say, the pair should be conditioned properly before a spawning is attempted. Being a large fish with a mouth and appetite to match, large chunks of food are preferred: pieces of raw shrimp, clams, mussels, snails and even smaller fish which are no longer wanted are just the thing. Some people

The free-swimming Oscar fry stays close to the parent for a certain length of time and gradually the bond weakens.

remove the breeders and let the young fend for themselves. Baby brine shrimp are an excellent first food and later when they begin to grow, live Daphnia and chopped Tubifex worms are eaten eagerly. If their bellies are kept full, growth is very rapid. The baby colors are a far cry from the mature coloration: there are many yellowish to white spots and streaks on a dark background, and not until about 3 to 4 inches in length are attained does the body become a rusty brown with red markings.

A young Oscar with a body length of an inch and a half still shows the juvenile pattern that will be replaced gradually with the typical pattern of the adult.

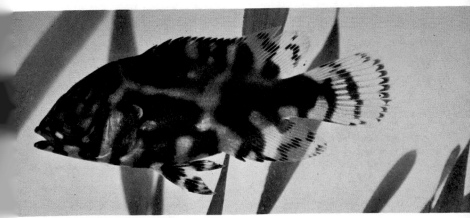

The Discus

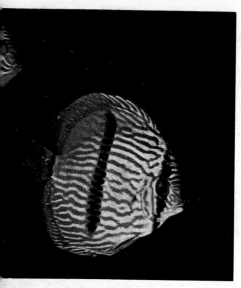

Symphysodon discus.

Symphysodon aequifasciata
axelrodi, *the Brown Discus.*

For many years the majestic
Discus fish species were
considered impossible to spawn
and resisted all efforts made at
coaxing them to do this. Many
were the trials, and many the
failures. Finally some heartening
progress was reported: here and
there people told of how their
Discus were laying eggs. Mostly
the parents would eat the eggs
shortly afterward, and so the
same technique was resorted to
as is the standard with Angelfish
breeding: the parents were
removed after spawning and an
airstone was placed so that it
would cause a gentle agitation of
the water nearby. This permitted
hatching all right and the
youngsters grew to a point where
their yolk sacs were absorbed,
but here the breeders ran into a

Symphysodon aequifasciata haraldi, *the Blue Discus.*

brick wall. The fry firmly and steadily refused to eat! Finally it was found that Discus babies had to be left in the care of their parents. They would then "graze" off the sides of the breeders and grow very well on this slime for about a week, after which time they could be fed newly-hatched brine shrimp.

To spawn this most majestic of all tropical fishes, plan to set up your spawning tank in the winter and early spring months. A tank of 50 to 100 gallons capacity is best. Of course you must have a ripe, healthy pair. Sexes are difficult to tell apart, but the male

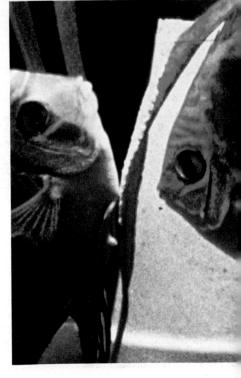

Note the extended ovipositor of this female Discus poised to add the next egg to the clutch while her partner is attentively watching.

Discus fry grazing on their parent's skin secretion.

is generally provided a little more generously with blue wavy lines on the sides. The water must be soft, about 2 or 3 DH, and slightly acid, pH about 6.5, and the temperature kept about 82° F. The breeders should be fed all sorts of living and freeze-dried foods to be brought into condition. It has been found most feasible to dispense with the bottom gravel, and set up the tank as it would be for Angelfish, with a strip of slate about 2 inches wide leaning against one side. Plants may be added in shallow pots, if desired. The pair swim up and down this slate, cleaning it off very meticulously. Finally you will see them side by side, the female laying strings of eggs and the male fertilizing them. When her egg-laying duties are done, the female assumes a position over them and waves her fins vigorously, circulating the water. This job is generally shared

The blurred appearance of the fry in this picture indicates they can move quite fast when disturbed, by a photo flash in this case.

by the pair, one fanning while the other stands guard. Hatching takes place in about 50 to 60 hours. The young are able to swim freely in a few days, at which time they begin to feed off either parent. An amusing tactic to watch is to observe the parent with the young attached when he

With faster growth in body depth than body length, the elongate young Discus develop into the shape typical of the adult.

(or she) figures it is time to take a rest. The other partner is approached and with a quick shuddering motion the youngsters are left behind to graze on the other one. The young Discus attain their disc shape in about 3 months, and at an age of 5 to 7 months their colors become evident. Maturity is not attained for at least 2 years.

The breeders should be left with the fry for about 2 to 3 weeks. To condition the breeders, feed them heavily on beef heart and live foods. At least 20 percent of their aquarium water should be siphoned off and replaced each week; 5 percent a day is even better.

The Blunthead Cichlid

Aequidens curviceps

This attractive fish is a most peaceful member of the Cichlid family. For this reason it does very nicely in a community tank. The Blunthead Cichlid, as it is sometimes called, is pleasingly colored. It has a brownish green back and silver gray sides with lovely iridescent sheens. The anal and caudal fins are yellow, speckled with bright blue dots. The female is lighter in color than her mate.

This fish comes from the Amazon River system. It grows to an average length of 3 inches and will start breeding at 2½ inches. It is relatively easy to sex this species. The male has pointed dorsal and anal fins. The dorsal has a red spot at the tip. The female's fins lack points and are much rounder.

The water should average between 74° and 83° F. for breeding, although temperature is not as critical as it is for other species. It should be soft and range from neutral to slightly acid (pH 6.5-7.0). For breeding, a well-planted aquarium is necessary; Amazon Swordplants, Giant *Sagittaria* and *Vallisneria* are preferred. The aquarium need not be large, about ten gallons, but should be supplied with several large flat stones and a flowerpot placed on its side in a corner.

Before spawning a stone will be chosen, cleaned and polished. The Amazon Swordplant may sometimes be chosen. There is

A Blunthead Cichlid in the process of cleaning the spawning substrate.

58

no obvious courtship. Eggs are
relatively large and range in
number from 100 to 200.

These fish are heavy feeders
and require more food than
usually would be expected for
their size, especially when they
are young. They prefer freeze-
dried foods such as Tubifex
worms, liver, meat and brine
shrimp, but will also eat dry food.

Prior to spawning their color
deepens. They start breeding at
four to five months. After
conditioning they should be
placed in a tank by themselves.
They are shy and need privacy
and are aggressive only at
spawning time. The pair will
select a spawning site. When they
are ready to spawn a small white
breeding tube will appear from
the anal pore; in the female this is
used to deposit the eggs. After
the site is carefully cleaned the
male will lure or sometimes drive
the female to the spot. She circles
with her tube passing along the

*The courtship is over, the
important phase of breeding is
about to start, that is, releasing
the first batch of eggs.*

surface leaving several curved
rows of eggs, numbering about
100.

One problem in breeding this
fish is their bad habit of eating
their first spawning completely
(rarely an exception). This may
also happen to the second; after
that, however, things go quite well
unless the parents are disturbed.
They take meticulous care of their
brood, taking turns at fanning and
occasionally mouthing the eggs
and newly hatched fry. The eggs
hatch 48-55 hours after spawning.
Then a fascinating thing happens!
The male takes each youngster
into his mouth and transfers it to
a hollow which had previously
been prepared. The mother will

The eggs are arranged in the shape of a circle, eggs produced earlier at the center, later ones at the periphery.

stand watch over the unhatched eggs. The fry are often transferred again to another depression usually seven days after hatching. The fry swim in short hops at first. They are free-swimming by the seventh day. The first feeding should be yolk of a hard-boiled egg squeezed through a cheese-cloth square, Infusoria, or brine shrimp. The pair may often spawn again, and will take turns caring for each brood. When the fry are able to swim about freely and care for themselves the parents are apt to eat them. It is advisable to remove the parents as soon as the fry are free-swimming. Up to this time the young are safe unless the parents are frightened. Although they are somewhat difficult to breed the results make it a worthwhile experience.

Transferring the fry by mouth into a pit or depression on the bottom is one of the chores of the male Blunthead Cichlid.

The Agassizi

Two male Agassizis sparring for superiority. This will lead to jaw-locking, but the weaker individual ultimately withdraws.

Apistogramma agassizi

Agassizi Dwarf Cichlids, from the Amazon Basin, are fairly peaceful, except when spawning, and are therefore quite suitable for a community aquarium. Their body coloration varies from a light yellowish brown to a bluish gray. The sides have a light blue lustre and are divided by a horizontal line which extends from the snout to the tip of the tail.

To enhance the chance of your Agassizi spawning, create a cave-like situation like the one shown here or something similar to it.

The male Agassizi averages 3 inches and begins breeding at 2 inches; the female is 1 inch smaller. Although they are one of the largest of the Dwarf Cichlids they don't require a large tank for breeding (5-10 gallons), but should be accommodated with many retreats. The breeding tank should be well planted.

The water should be fairly soft and almost neutral. Temperature

However, Agassizis will not hesitate to spawn on flat rocks at times. The male is seen here waiting to fertilize the eggs.

This photo shows the size difference between the male and female Apistogramma agassizi. *In spite of her small size, she will be able to drive the male off later.*

should range between 72° and 85°F., averaging about 78°F. When conditioning them it is better to reduce the temperature to 76° F. They are carnivorous. Tubifex worms are preferred.

The female has a round tail. She is yellowish in color; her fins are brownish. The male is the more colorful and his dorsal, anal and ventral fins are bluish with bright orange to red on the borders. The tail fin comes to a center point and is black. Prior to spawning the colors become very bright in both sexes.

This species is not particularly easy to breed. They are egg hiders, often placing eggs out of sight in pockets between rocks. Place a small flowerpot on its side in a dark corner and spawning will usually take place either in or underneath it. The male will scoop out a hole under the flowerpot by spitting out a few grains at a time, working over a spot until it suits him. The female is then sought and if not ready for spawning she may get badly beaten.

When *A. agassizi* are ready to spawn their color darkens. A small tube appears at their anal pore, which in the female is twice the diameter of the male's. If they are not disturbed, spawning will usually take place the next day. The female is coy at first but is finally coaxed to the spawning site where the eggs are deposited in a group. In the beginning she passes over the spawning site a few times and nothing happens; but soon she begins to leave a trail of eggs behind, until 50-150 are deposited. The male follows and fertilizes the eggs. This species often eats its eggs or fry, so to assure safe hatching artificial methods are advised. The oval eggs are a yellow or brownish red. After mating, the

previously shy female becomes a virtual lioness. She chases the male away, fiercely attacking and biting him, and takes care of the brood herself. It is best to remove the male at this point. The fry hatch in about four days and will lie helplessly squirming on the bottom. It takes three days for the yolk sac to be absorbed and the fry to become free-swimming. Until they are able to swim, they are hidden by their mother in previously dug out pits or clefts between stones. They are moved about from hole to hole several times during this period. She stays and fans them continually with her pectoral fins. She will often take them into her mouth

Another pair of Agassizis that was provided with a split half of coconut shell as a spawning substrate. Coconut shells are rarely used today; they are not always easily available and unless properly prepared can pollute the water.

and cleanse them and then spit them out again. It was observed that many spawnings were lost if the female was removed prior to the free-swimming stage. When the fry become free-swimming the female becomes darker. It was found that in most broods there were more males then females. A pre-spawning kiss has occasionally been observed in this species.

The Kribensis

Pelvicachromis pulcher

Most of the African Cichlid species are quite large in size, and there are not many that could be considered dwarf species. *Pelvicachromis pulcher* is small enough to come into this category. In addition to their not-above-medium size both sexes are among the most beautifully colored of all freshwater species.

The female is about half the size of the male. The bottom half of her head is a greenish yellow and most of her much shorter dorsal fin is a golden yellow. The belly has a wine-red area like the male's.

When provided with conditions to their liking, a well-mated pair of these fish will spawn with regularity. One of the most successful methods has been to set a flowerpot with its open end on the bottom. A piece is broken out of the side to permit both fish to swim in and out, and the temperature is set at 80°F. They

When not actively breeding, the male Kribensis assumes a neutral coloration, but the color pattern stays recognizable. Photo by J. Voss.

Facing page: upper photo: *Presumably, the colorful appearance of a fish when guarding its young serves as means of keeping the fry close to the parent.*

begin exploring in short order. Soon you will notice that they are spending a great deal of time in the flowerpot, and then one day you will see the male come pell-mell out of the opening, with the indignant female sticking her head out to make sure he doesn't come back. This is the right time to take the male out and give the

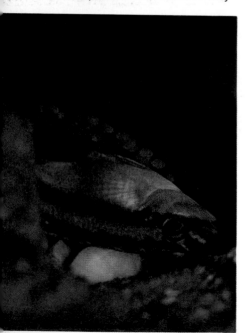

Spawning and brooding will take place in a hidden site; the breeders could remain unseen until the female Kribensis takes the fry out in the open.

female a chance to tend her eggs. The eggs hatch in 2 to 3 days, and the fry become free-swimming 3 to 5 days after that. When you see the female leading her brood out of the flowerpot it is time to feed the youngsters. At this point you can play it safe and remove the female because the youngsters can take care of themselves, or you can keep the female with them and watch her herding her brood and keeping them in a close group. The gamble here is that she could suddenly turn on her own young and eat them. The hardboiled yolk of a chicken egg, squeezed through a cloth, makes a good starter food if not fed too

generously. In a few days they will be able to consume newly-hatched brine shrimp. From here on it is just a matter of keeping the little bellies filled.

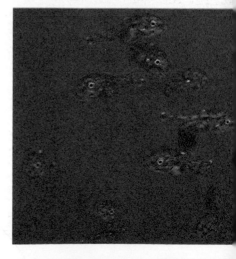

The yolk sac is used up gradually and the fry must be fed or it will gradually starve.

The Egyptian Mouthbrooder

Pseudocrenilabrus multicolor
These dwarf Egyptian mouthbrooders have been imported into England and the United States from North and East Africa since about the turn of the century. They were once known as *Haplochromis multicolor* but were renamed as

A male Egyptian Mouthbrooder in breeding coloration.

metallic sheen speckled with golds, greens, blues and purples. If frightened or disturbed various splotches and bands become quite distinct. The gill covers are green, decorated with black and edged posteriorly in gold. The dorsals are a brownish red. The tail is a yellowish-green. As is true of many species, the males are endowed with the greater beauty. Sex is easily determined. The most obvious indication is the proportionally larger head structure, especially the mouth, of

their genus was further studied. Although their disposition seems to vary from one individual to another, they can usually be kept in a community tank.

Egyptian mouthbrooders are not particularly sensitive to their water conditions. Neutral, slightly hard (12 DH) water and temperatures between 65° and 80°F. with an optimum around 72°F. seems to suit them best. The tank should be well lit and stocked with many plants and rocks. Their diet should include a variety of living food.

The males will attain a size up to 3 inches, the females somewhat smaller; both breed at about half their full length. Their body varies from a pale yellow to almost a bronze. The scales along the back and sides reflect a

the female. Colorwise she is a drab clay with several indistinct splotches running across her body; her fins are nearly transparent and colorless. The male boasts a rainbow of colors, and numerous iridescent sheens, depending upon the light. During the breeding season he has a bright orange spot on his anal fin. The other unpaired fins have several rows of dots.

Their usual courtship and subsequent fry care are fascinating to observe. A small tank of about six gallons is all that is necessary. Divide it into two equal parts with a glass partition and cover the bottom with about 1½ inches of fine, non-sharp gravel. Plants are usually uprooted. A flowerpot is provided for a hiding place, especially if the tank lacks

A female Egyptian Mouthbrooder that is very full of eggs.

plants as this will give the breeders some security and will put them more at ease. Filtration and aeration are not necessary. Separation of sexes by a partition in the breeding tank will ensure greater success since they can be brought into the proper condition more readily and you can manipulate the time to ensure that they are both ready. The partition allows them to see one another and consequently hastens things along.

With a rise in temperature to about 77°F. the male will almost immediately take on his brilliant mating colors. After copious feedings of live foods, especially Tubifex and brine shrimp, the abdomen of the female will begin to bulge. The male will flaunt his elegant colors, fins spread, back

and forth along the partition. He will begin to actively excavate a shallow depression about 3 inches in diameter in one of the corners. The fine gravel is picked up and removed by mouthfuls. When this has been completed, remove the partition. He begins to dance again, swimming about in circles, coaxing and butting the female until she agrees to follow him. Occasionally he may lock jaws in a pre-spawning kiss; there is seldom any damage. They will break apart and continue to slowly circle one another over the hollow, periodically nudging the other's abdomen. During this time the male may make some minor repairs or adjustments on the nest. After a number of incomplete matings, a few eggs are released. The female will gently butt her mate as he fertilizes them, and then carefully gathers them into her mouth. The whole process will be repeated until the sac in her throat is bulging, and she retreats. This is the signal to remove the male.

One more egg to pick up! Sometimes for no apparent cause a female Egyptian Mouthbrooder may swallow the eggs or spit them out.

motion. The eggs are incubated for 10 to 14 days in her mouth. During this time she will not accept any food. After hatching the fry will begin to venture outside their mother's mouth for short periods but if they feel threatened they will quickly swim back in. They are gathered up each night and sleep in their mother's mouth. Incubation and the time until they are free swimming are both controlled by temperature; the higher the temperature the shorter the time. Four to five days after they are free-swimming the female should be removed. By this time she has lost some of her maternal instincts, and hunger becoming the stronger drive, she might turn and eat them.

The eggs are small and brownish, and number from 30 to 100. The mother keeps fresh water circulating through her mouth with a slow chewing

The brooding instinct will wane gradually and the female Egyptian Mouthbrooder is best removed before she starts feeding on her own fry.

The Dwarf Pencil Fish

Nannostomus marginatus
The Dwarf Pencil Fish from Guyana are perfect for a community aquarium of smaller fishes. They reach a maximum length of about 1½ inches and will breed at 1¼ inches. They will accept most types of food. Their water may be neutral to slightly acid but they need warmth, so temperatures should range between 75° and 85°F.

Three dark horizontal bands traverse the body separated by intermediate golden lines. The dorsal and ventral fins have a red blotch which adds the needed spark of color. The sexes are not easy to distinguish except for the heavier, more robust appearance of the female.

To breed, fill a five gallon tank with five inches of clear, aged water which is soft and slightly

When ready to spawn the male Dwarf Pencil Fish will drive his mate relentlessly all over the tank.

These popular little fish are the smallest of their genus. They are endowed with fairly attractive coloration. Their back is a dark brown which becomes silvery along the sides and abdomen.

acid. Provide a clump of fine-leaved plants *(Nitella, Riccia,* or *Myriophyllum).* Separate the sexes until the male has acquired a greater intensity of color and the female is bulging with roe. After an active romp about the tank, the eggs are deposited in among the plants near the surface of the water. Unfortunately they have a fondness for their own eggs and

Butting the female at the side is typical breeding behavior.

the trick is to save the eggs before they have eaten the entire spawning. Various traps are employed for this purpose. A layer of glass rods, suspended an inch above the bottom will allow the eggs to fall through and will separate them from the breeders. Spawnings are small and average about 50. The fry will begin to hatch in about 72 hours if kept at a constant 78°F. They are extremely small at first and for this reason frequently starve. They must be fed the smallest Infusoria.

With vents close together, the partners release the genital products simultaneously.

The Neon Tetra

Paracheirodon innesi

The Neon Tetras have long been one of the best known and most popular of all tropical fishes, and are frequently referred to as the aristocrats of the small aquarium specimens. They inhabit the streams of the Peruvian Amazon near Iquitos, and Yarapa River where they travel about in schools, sometimes reaching into the hundreds of thousands. The natives in this region used to gather up as many of these as they could into a jar, or whatever they had, and went to the trading post of Rafael Wanderraga where they obtained cigarettes, clothing or canned goods for a specific number of Neons. Enormous numbers of Neon Tetras are imported yearly.

Neons come from waters which are nearly void of minerals, being derived to a large extent from rain water. Their colors are brought out to the fullest in water which is soft, clear and slightly acid, with a temperature between 72° and 76°F. Their tank should be neatly

Neons are one of the most often recommended fish for a community tank. They are small but truly very colorful fish.

planted with a dark gravel bottom to offset their bright flashy colors. They reach a maximum of 1½ inches but the majority are 1 inch or less. Their colors are magnificent and a school of Neons racing about catching beams of sunlight is quite a sight. The colorful part of their body is a dark maroon, transversed by a shiny bluish green stripe which extends from the eye to the base of the adipose fin. This line is straight in the males and slightly crooked in the egg-filled females. The belly is silvery becoming a bright red in the posterior half of the body through the caudal peduncle. The fins are transparent and colorless. They are not fussy eaters and will eagerly accept brine shrimp and other meaty foods. When

The Neon Tetra

Active chase indicates the start of possible spawning of Neon Tetras.

attempting to breed this species, choose an attractively colored pair which is over nine months old. Condition on ample helpings of the aforementioned foods. A five gallon breeding tank which is completely glass and dimly lit should be provided with several bunches of rinsed plants. Water conditions are particularly important at this time. The water should be very soft, no more than 3 DH, acid (pH 6.5), with a temperature ranging about 73° to 74°F. with the addition of two teaspoons of salt to each gallon. The tank must be kept clean, and

Spawning can occur anywhere, but generally it takes place over a bushy plant.

Lacking parental care behavior, Neons can eat their eggs the moment they are released.

there should be light aeration. When the female has become swollen with roe, place the pair into the breeding tank. If there aren't any spawning activities within two days remove and condition them a few more days on more generous feedings of live foods. Spawning consists of an active chase through the plant thickets. About 60 to 130 non-adhesive eggs are scattered throughout the tank. Remove the breeders when spawning is completed and cover the tank until the eggs hatch, since they are very sensitive to light. They hatch in about a day. Keep them covered until the fifth day when they are free-swimming, then increase the light gradually. Feed them the yolk of hard boiled egg squeezed through a porous cloth. Unfortunately even after much care few survive. Nearly all specimens sold are imported.

The Red-bellied Piranha

Serrasalmus nattereri

The Red-bellied Piranhas are one of the most respected of all fresh water fishes. They have a wide distribution in the rivers and streams throughout the Amazon and Orinoco Basins. They are

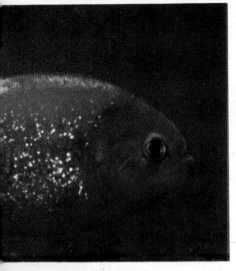

The characteristic red belly and silvery scales are very evident in this adult Red-bellied Piranha.

quite vicious and should be kept alone in an average sized tank or in a large tank if in a pair. They are accustomed to swimming in schools and seem to lose their boldness when by themselves. When isolated they become nervous and are easily startled so it is best to provide them with numerous retreats including several floating aquatic plants and perhaps a piece of driftwood. The water requirements are quite flexible, though they seem to prefer temperatures between 75° and 82°F.

They have powerful jaws armed with razor sharp, interlocking triangular teeth. Their face is blunt with a bulldog-like muzzle. They may reach a length of a foot

or so in their natural environment but rarely reach that size in captivity. They are carnivorous and have tremendous appetites. They will chop a smaller fish in half and swallow the portion whole. Large quantities of live fish and chunks of fresh meat make up the bulk of their diet. It seems they are always hungry.

Their body is a steel blue while the throat, abdomen and anal fin are a glowing red. There are numerous shining red and green scales scattered along the back and sides. It is not particularly easy to determine the sex of these fish. It is believed that the female is the larger of the pair with more subdued coloration and a deeper body.

Although actual spawning of piranhas in captivity is relatively rare, a few breeders have had success. Choose a healthy pair about 6 inches in length and condition them on generous amounts of live fish or pieces of meat. Prepare a large breeding tank (100 gallons or larger) with Water Sprite and other floating aquatics and place it where the breeders will not be disturbed. If they are compatible they will

Many eggs are produced and they stick to the spawning grass. However, a few of them will fail to develop; the opaque ones were possibly not fertilized at all.

Trembling and quivering accompany the last phases of spawning. Red-bellied Piranhas are large in size, very active during breeding, and should be bred in a fairly large aquarium.

swim curiously around one another, taking occasional nips in pre-spawning play. They will begin to swim in a side-by-side position assuming a less aggressive manner. Their color deepens. Their body becomes a dark gray and their fins turn black. The pair begin to slowly circle one another, one occasionally slapping the other with its tail. They come up under a plant which is resting on the surface and somersault, with their bodies trembling in close contact as the eggs begin to flow. The male has his anal fin positioned over the vent of the female and the sperm is also released while in this upside down position. The translucent eggs adhere to the plants or they are eaten. Care varies with the individual couple. The eggs are sometimes carefully guarded, other times ignored or eaten. Some mouthing has been observed. The fry will hatch in two to four days and will hang suspended by a thread in a horizontal position. It is another nine days until they are free swimming. At this time they are about a half inch long and will eagerly accept brine shrimp and after several days, small white worms.

The juvenile Red-bellied Piranha possesses a distinctly spotted pattern. The adults being large, the fish available to an aquarist will most likely be a juvenile.

The Tiger Barb

Capoeta tetrazona

These fish from Sumatra and Borneo were listed as *Barbus tetrazona* or *Puntius tetrazona* until Dr. L. P. Schultz divided up the classification of Barbs according to the number of barbels they possess.

The Tiger Barbs are frisky and very fast swimmers, and are inclined to playfully nip the fins of slower species. For this reason they should not be kept with long-finned species such as Bettas or thread-finned fishes such as Gouramis or Angelfish. They do best if kept in schools.

Although they can reach a size of 3 inches, most range about 2 inches, the size at which they breed. They have excellent appetites and will eat both live and prepared foods. They are semi-scavengers in that they will gobble up the uneaten food on the bottom and vegetative matter in the dirt which other species would refuse to eat. They need a good and varied diet; an overlooked item will prevent them from reaching maturity. If well fed their bellies will always appear swollen.

C. tetrazona are good aquarium fish because they are hardy and their flashy colors make them one of the most beautiful of the Barbs. Their sides are a golden pink with four wide, very black stripes. Their dorsal fin is black with the

Tiger Barbs look good when kept in a group in the community tank where one can enjoy observing their habits, including breeding behavior.

This strain of Tiger Barb has lost most of the dark pigments, except in the iris of the eye. The body bands are no longer black.

upper border neatly trimmed in red. The upper and lower lobes of the tail and ventral fins are red with the scales elegantly edged with a shining gold. The male has a bright red nose when mature and in spawning condition.

They should be kept in 10- to 15-gallon tanks which are well planted and have a dark bottom. There should be moderate lighting with some direct sunlight in part of the tank. This promotes the growth of algae which is

The opposite has occurred in this Tiger Barb; more dark pigment developed beyond the normal width of the transverse bands.

The Tiger Barb

eaten and enhances their color. The tank must be well oxygenated and kept free of droppings because this species is especially sensitive to fouling water. The water should be soft and slightly acid. The temperature can range from 70° to 85°F. with a good overall temperature of 74°F. Breeding will start when this is raised to 78° to 80°F.

clump of fine-leaved plants (Myriophyllum). Spanish moss and nylon yarn are also suitable if they are boiled before they are used and then pulled apart so the fish can easily swim in and out of them. The temperature should be raised to 78° to 80°F. Early the next morning spawning begins. It is fascinating to watch the lively chase which takes place. The

This species is easy to breed; they spawn in the typical Barb fashion. They should be separated for conditioning. The water should be softer than usual and aged at least three days. They must be fed a copious amount of foods. The sexes can easily be distinguished. The male has the characteristic cherry red nose and the female is less brilliantly colored with a heavier body. They are ready to spawn when the female has a noticeable bulge in her abdomen and the colors of the male have deepened.

They should be placed in a large tank on the evening before a day you wish them to breed. One-third of the tank should contain a

Two Tiger Barbs showing interest in each other. The fish at the right is a ripe female; her abdomen is quite prominent.

male may nip at the anal fins of the female. In some instances this may be severe enough to be fatal to her. Soon the female will slow down and let the male catch up. They come into a trembling side-by-side position in among the plants. Three to six eggs are expelled and immediately fertilized by the male. The chase then continues, the stops become more and more frequent, until all the eggs have been scattered throughout the tank. The breeders should be removed as

Artificial spawning grass serves to catch the eggs of these breeding Tiger Barbs.

soon as possible because they immediately commence an egg hunt and gobble up all they can find.

If the temperature is kept at 80°F., the fry will hatch in 48 hours and hang on the plants or the glass sides. The are small at first but growth is rapid if they have plenty of room. If kept in too

small a tank they will not attain full size. Infusoria is an excellent first food, supplemented with fry food and newly hatched brine shrimp.

Closeup view of the individual eggs stuck on the filaments of the spawning grass.

The Rosy Barb

Puntius conchonius
Rosy Barbs are a popular fish
which are nearly always available.
In their native India they may
reach a length of 6 inches;
however in captivity they seldom
exceed 3½ inches. Hardy and
undemanding, they will accept
any type of aquarium food they
are offered but do best on freeze-
dried foods. They are continually
hungry, perhaps because they are
such active, untiring swimmers.
When you pass their aquarium

*A normal variety of Rosy Barb
that one finds in the aquarium
hobby.*

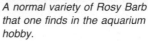

you will notice them constantly
racing back and forth in groups of
six or more. Their tank should be
long and low with plenty of
swimming area and numerous
plants. Temperature should be
kept around 72° to 76° F.

*The longfinned type has the
normal colors of the common
variety.*

*The male Rosy Barb is easy to
distinguish by its deep rosy red
color.*

They are usually a shiny silvery shade with a dark black mark on the caudal peduncle which is neatly trimmed in gold; the back is an iridescent olive-green. As spawning approaches, the males develop a bright red glow in their bodies and tails, with the fins tipped in a deep black. The females acquire a gentle blush, making it easy to distinguish the sexes.

This species is very prolific and will spawn readily if well conditioned. They need a fairly large tank and have even been known to spawn in an outdoor pool. A pair will chase around the tank and finally dash into the plant bundles scattering the eggs.

They tolerate the cold well and are raised in outdoor pools in Florida.

Longfinned Rosy Barbs were developed in Russia, but they are now available in many countries.

Rosy Barbs continually search for food at the bottom of the tank, so any eggs within reach are devoured.

The Zebra Danio

Brachydanio rerio

The Zebra or Striped Danio, as these fish are commonly called, are native to the small, swiftly moving streams of the Coromandel Coast of India. They are ideal for a community aquarium since they are hardy, attractive and quite peaceful. They are full of energy and although extremely active, their movements are graceful. They prefer to swim in schools.

A gravid Zebra Danio female, quite ready to spawn.

In addition to the common Zebra Danio shown here, there is a longfinned variety, perhaps a bit more costly, available today.

They are one of the most popular and easily kept tropical aquarium fish. Their appearance is quite striking. The female reaches about 2 inches, the male is slender and somewhat smaller. The body is silvery, sometimes tinted with gold, with seven to nine blue horizontal stripes which are also present in the anal and caudal fins. The male is striped in

between the blue with gold while in the female these are silver.

Providing these perky little fish with adequate environmental conditions is no problem. Their water may range from slightly acid (6.6) to slightly alkaline (7.2); hardness is not important as long as it isn't extreme. They have an unusual temperature range and are capable of tolerating water between 60° and 110°F., with an optimum of about 75°F. Fill their tank with clean tap water which is kept well aerated. They have hardy appetites and accept all

chance to hatch. Several methods may be used. One employs a fine-meshed grating or false bottom suspended an inch or so above the bottom so the eggs can drop down out of their parents' reach. Another method suggests a layer of dark marbles so the eggs can fall in between and later be siphoned off.

Choose at least a 5-gallon tank which is long and shallow and supply it with numerous bushy plants and a good amount of light. Select a number of one year old specimens which are about

Female Zebra Danios will spawn with different males at different times.

aquarium foods although their diet should include some live foods.

Spawning *B. rerio* is not difficult and they are quite prolific; however precautions must be taken to prevent the eggs from being eaten before they have a

1½ inches long and separate the sexes for about a week to ten days. Condition these selected breeders with four to five daily feedings of choice foods such as Tubifex worms and brine shrimp.

When they appear in proper condition, that is, the females are full and the males are active and colorful, place them into the breeding tank. A ratio of two males to each female should be used. Daybreak appears to be an adequate stimulus and spawning will occur early in the morning;

then there will be a mad, hectic chase about the aquarium. Two fish will press close together as they swim and the eggs will be released and fertilized. They will continue to spawn at regular intervals; the female will be ripe again in three weeks. Remove the breeders immediately after spawning, before they have a chance to search for the eggs. If this is the female's first mating, the first spawning will probably not hatch, but the second will and each succeeding spawn will be larger and more fertile. The semi-adhesive eggs are large and clear

A long-finned variety of Zebra Danio, also easy to breed, is now available to hobbyists.

and average about 200 in number. They hatch in about 24 to 36 hours and the fry are free-swimming in about two days. They are easily raised. Give them plenty of room and food. They may cling to the sides of the tank and plant leaves. They are mature in four to six months. Feed the fry newly-hatched brine shrimp.

Note the eggs just released by this pair of Zebra Danio.

The Harlequin

Rasbora heteromorpha

The *Rasbora* has long been considered one of the most popular as well as one of the most beautiful aquarium fishes, and its propagation has been the despair of many breeders. There is an interesting story in this connection. In Germany it was found that breeders in certain parts of Saxony had very little trouble breeding this little beauty, while highly skilled experts in other parts of the same country found it practically impossible to get any but the most meager results. It was believed that the Saxony breeders were in possession of some deep, dark secret which enabled them to breed *Rasboras* with ease using no more than fresh, clean water. A test of this water was made, and the answer to the puzzle was found. Water in this district was not only unusually soft, but also quite strongly acid. The same water, by coincidence, also gave good results in the breeding of Neon Tetras.

A female Harlequin. The extent of the marking on the side of the body could vary slightly among different individuals.

The secret of success, then, lies in the use of the proper kind of water. Strange, isn't it, that the same water properties should lead to spawnings in two fish, one from Malaysia and the other in the upper Amazon River in Peru?

To arrive at this utopian water condition, begin by cleaning out a tank of about 2 gallons capacity. Fill this tank with clean rain water, then throw in two handfuls or so of acid peat moss. In the course of three weeks to a month, most of the peat moss will have settled to the bottom. Then it is time to prepare your breeding tank, which should be approximately 10 gallons in size and also carefully cleaned out. Remove the water which has been standing for a month with the peat moss in it by siphoning it into another clean

The Harlequin

container, being careful to leave the peat moss behind. Then boil the peat moss, using fresh, clean rain water. This is then spread over the botom of the breeding tank. Then add the rain water which had been standing with the peat moss in it, and then a few broad-leaved *Cryptocoryne* plants, which may be planted in well-cleaned flowerpots. To avoid

Harlequins are very attractive. They are good community tank fish, too.

stirring up the water pour the water over a bowl or a flat rock. The rest of the tank is then filled with distilled water, checking frequently until a pH of 5.5 to 5.7 is attained. The DH should be about 3. The fish are then added, making sure the temperature has been equalized, after which the temperature is gradually brought up to 80°F.

If you have a ripe breeding pair, the male will soon begin driving the female all over the tank, "riding" atop the female's back. Soon she will take an upside-down position under one of the broad leaves and wait for the male to swim up to her and wrap his body about hers while she releases a number of eggs and hangs them from the underside of the leaf. This procedure is

This male Harlequin is poised to get on the back of this ripe female and lead her to the spawning site.

The most common site selected is the underside of a broad leaf where the eggs are attached.

frequently repeated until her supply of eggs has become exhausted. Once in a while a few fall into the layer of peat moss, which does not prevent them from hatching. When spawning is finished, the parents should be removed and the tank darkened by putting a newspaper or towel over it. The eggs hatch in one day and the fry become free-swimming five days later. The newspaper or towel may then be removed and feeding begun. They have good appetites and will take any food they can swallow. They can be easily fed on a bit of hard-boiled egg yolk squeezed through a clean cloth, or newly-hatched brine shrimp. Growth is quite rapid.

Condition the breeders with brine shrimp, meat, liver and Tubifex worms.

In the frenzy of breeding some of the eggs are not attached to the substrate, but fall and hatch elsewhere.

The White Cloud

Tanichthys albonubes

White Clouds are native to the swiftly flowing mountain streams of Hong Kong and Canton, China. Their generic name, *Tanichthys*, means "Tan's fish," for they were named after a Chinese Boy Scout who discovered them in 1938 in the White Cloud Mountains. They are a perfect aquarium fish and ideal for beginners since they are extremely hardy and are easy to keep and spawn. They are very active and prefer to swim in schools. Their demands on their

A variety of White Cloud with long fins, at times called Meteor Minnows.

Color pattern of the regular White Cloud.

environment are few. They come from cold, clear waters which frequently carry melted snow down into the valleys. Keep them in an unheated aquarium at temperatures between 62° and 70° F. They can withstand temperatures down to 50°F., but when they rise above 80° F. the fish become weak and soon die. Place the tank so that it receives good lighting and supply it with numerous plants. The pH may range from 6.5 to 7.5. Their water should be kept clear, since

they are rather sensitive to foul
water. They have a small mouth
and being omnivorous will accept
all foods if they are not too large
for them to swallow.

These fish reach a length of
about 1½ inches. Their body is an
olive green. There is a reddish
gold stripe which runs across the
body and terminates in a black
spot at the base of the tail. Just
beneath this runs another
greenish stripe. The belly is a
dusty white. The dorsal and anal
fins are a pale yellow becoming
deep red along the border. The
tail is a beautiful bright red. The
female is the larger and fuller
partner. Her colors are somewhat
subdued compared to the male's.

They are eager breeders and
are probably the simplest
egglaying fish to spawn. Choose a
pair which is about a year old.
Separate the sexes and condition
them on generous feedings of live
foods for about a week. Prepare a
medium-sized aquarium by
supplying a layer of
numerous fine-leaved plants

*A male White Cloud starting to
chase the female from behind.
The male White Cloud continues
to drive the female to the
spawning site.*

*The female White Cloud almost
ready to "explode" being driven to
the spawning site by the male.*

(Fontinalis, Elodea, Nitella, or
Myriophyllum) and regular tap
water. Place it in a sunny spot for
about a week and a half.

Spawning will take place at
temperatures between 72° and
75° F. Courting is fascinating to
watch. The male does a graceful
dance with his fins widely spread.
If the female seems unconcerned
he will nudge or butt her in the
abdomen with his snout.
Presently she will search for a
spawning site. The male will swim
up alongside her and while their
bodies are pressing against one
another the male will gently
embrace the female. The non-
adhesive eggs will be scattered
among the plants where they are
fertilized. They are released
singly. Mating continues at
frequent intervals. There is no
need to remove the breeders

*At the spawning site the male
White Cloud wraps his body
around the female's dorsal fin.
Within a couple of seconds the
eggs will be released and fall
toward the bottom.*

after spawning has been
completed. The transparent eggs
are very small and few in number.
They hatch in 24 hours and the fry
are free-swimming in 4 to 6 days.
Supply them with small Infusoria
or fine dry foods. Be careful to
keep conditions stable since they
are sensitive to water changes at
first. In the young the green stripe
is so bright that they are
frequently thought to be small
Neon Tetras. The parents usually
ignore the fry unless they are
hungry.

The Bronze Catfish

Corydoras aeneus

C. aeneus are probably the most popular and best known of the armored catfish. Their coloration is pleasing but by no means flashy. Their body is a yellowish to a greenish brown with a metallic glint on the sides; their belly is a grayish yellow.

These fish are found in shallow, muddy waters, frequently in shoals, all over a good part of South America, but most come from Trinidad. They are quite peaceful and, being willing scavengers of the bottom, are useful in keeping the tank free of uneaten particles of food which could foul the water. They may reach a size of 2¾ inches but usually are somewhat smaller in captivity. They accept any aquarium food, dried or prepared, but should be fed occasional Tubifex worms to keep them in top condition.

Their water should be fresh and neutral to slightly alkaline. A hardness of around 10 DH is best since calcium is needed for their

Closeup of the head of a Bronze Catfish with the barbels clearly in view. These organs are supplied with sensory cells for detecting food.

Courting can take place anywhere in the tank. This attitude, often called the T-position, is exhibited by many fishes during spawning.

In this instance a single egg was laid on a leaf. More eggs were to follow.

normal growth. They are native to waters of low oxygen content and have a form of intestinal respiration which helps to supplement the normal oxygen intake. They can be seen taking occasional gulps of air and then diving back down to the bottom. The intestines are lined with numerous tiny blood vessels and act much as a lung in osmotic respiratory exchange.

A female Bronze Catfish can also transfer eggs anywhere else with her pelvic fins.

These catfish are alert and often comical, always in constant motion, actively surveying the bottom. They have a double pair of barbels which are useful in the dark in getting about safely and locating food. These also serve as accessory taste organs and play a part in mating. They are well protected wih bony armor plates and so have little to fear, even from much larger fish.

Bronze catfish are very easily bred. The sexes should be separated while they are being conditioned and fed generous amounts of live foods, worms in particular. The male, the smaller, will take on an even more noticeable metallic sheen while his mate will acquire a reddish color on her belly. When the female is well rounded put her with one or two males in a bare tank of at least 15 gallons. Tap water may be used. Temperature is not important but breeding is more likely to take place if the tank temperature is raised to 80°F. and then overnight slowly allowed to fall to 60°F. This seems to provide the necessary stimulus. There will be a great deal of lively courting activity. The male will hover just above the female as he races back and forth across the tank continually trying to excite her by tickling her from all sides with his barbels. From time to time he will come into a position above her and attach his mouth to the back of her neck. They will swim around in this position for a while. If the female is ready to mate she starts looking for a spawning site and will begin cleaning a small surface area, usually on the glass. The male will then drop to the bottom and roll over onto his side. His mate swims down and attaches her mouth to his vent to receive his sperm. He grips her barbels

The eggs of the Bronze Catfish are adhesive and get stuck on any surface.

with the stiff rays of his pectoral fins. She curves her body slightly, releasing five to six large, pearly eggs into a small pocket formed by the folding together of her two ventral fins. She releases the male and swims up and touches the prepared site with her mouth, depositing the sperm onto the glass. She then pushes the tough, very adhesive eggs up against the same spot where they will adhere tightly until they hatch. The courting continues until all the eggs have been depleted (about

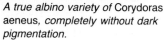

150) and the glass sides are completely covered. There is no animosity between rivals and one female may mate with a different male each time. After spawning

A true albino variety of Corydoras aeneus, *completely without dark pigmentation.*

the parents should be removed. The eggs will hatch in three to four days depending on the temperature (four days if a constant 75°F.). The fry will lie on the bottom, rather than clinging to the glass sides as do the fry of other egg-layers. At this stage they resemble tiny white tadpoles. In five days they will be free-swimming. They should be fed Infusoria, newly-hatched brine shrimp and microworms. Growth is rather slow. They will start to resemble their parents in color in about one month, being a mottled brown until then. They reach maturity in about two years.

There is another interpretation of how fertilization takes place, which has merit. It states that the female attaches herself to the belly of the male and that he releases the sperm in a cloud which envelops the couple. An albino variety exists.

The eggs are susceptible to fungus that will suffocate and kill them. Experienced breeders sometimes use fungicides for controlling fungal growth.

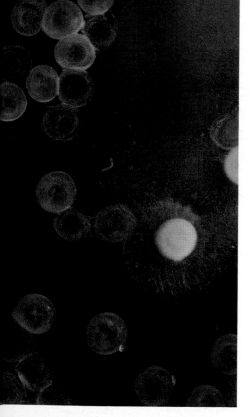

The Striped Panchax

Aplocheilus lineatus

The Killifishes are fairly well distributed throughout the world, and the *Aplocheilus* species of killifishes are native to parts of tropical Asia. Like many of the African Killifishes, they spawn among bushy plants and the eggs hatch in about 10 to 15 days. The Striped Panchax, as this one is called, is the most popular of the group.

Being a robust species which grows to 4 inches in length and with a large mouth, they should never be kept with other fishes which could conceivably be swallowed. In such cases you can often see a Striped Panchax swimming about with a smaller fish's tail protruding from its mouth!

Both sexes are very attractive, but the male has the brighter colors and larger fins. His sides are also adorned with rows of scales that have a bright gold area in the center. His tail often has a bright red margin above and below. The female has paler colors but has 7 vertical bars from the center of the body to the tail base. Another distinguishing mark is a black area at the lower part of the dorsal fin. This makes it practically impossible to make a mistake when sexing them.

A pair or trio consisting of a male and two females should be kept in a covered aquarium, because they are active jumpers. Best water for them is slightly acid and fairly soft (pH 6.8, DH about 5), and the temperature about 76°F. For breeding, an aquarium of 5 gallons has the advantage over a larger one in that the eggs are concentrated in a smaller space and are easier to find. A few strands of some bushy plant, preferably *Myriophyllum* are floated to receive the eggs. These can be removed when a

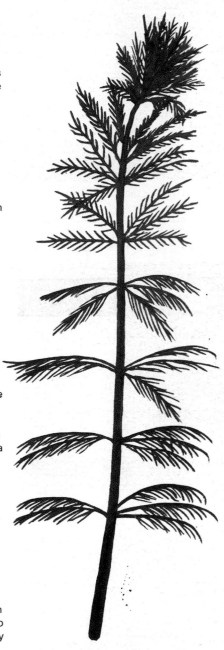

Myriophyllum *is available in almost any aquarium shop.*

good number of them can be seen, or if it is decided to continue using the plants the eggs can be removed with a pair of tweezers or the fingers. The eggs, like the *Aphyosemion* species', also withstand a certain amount of handling. The use of the "natural" method is not recommended, because the Striped Panchax is a fairly greedy proposition and would make short work of the fry when they hatched.

The fry are provided with marvelous appetites as soon as they hatch, and are constantly on the hunt for living newly-hatched brine shrimp. They grow at a rapid rate and are very hardy. Their only drawback is that they are reluctant to accept dry foods.

A phase of the hobby that receives little mention should be brought up here. The hatching period of approximately two

The black vertical bars are only developed in the female Striped Panchax.

weeks makes it possible to drop a few newly-laid eggs into a small vial of water, seal it and wrap so that it will be insulated, and air-mail it just about anywhere. This makes it possible for the recipient to complete the hatching process in his own tank and have the thrill of raising fish that were perhaps spawned thousands of miles away.

Facing page:
Striped Panchax are not fussy breeders. They can spawn any place that is convenient, perhaps on bushy plants near the surface or at the bottom on the gravel and among the rocks.

Although the newly hatched fry of some tropical fish species are too small to swallow entire brine shrimp nauplii, newly hatched Aplocheilus lineatus *fry have no such problem—they're plenty big enough to handle the crustaceans. Photo by Dr. Sylvan Cohen.*

The Lyretail

Aphyosemion australe
These lovely and popular Lyretails are native to the swampy, vegetation-clogged waters of the

A Lyretail male. Lyretails are variable and may differ slightly from individual to individual in color pattern.

The Lyretail eggs attached to this spawning mop may be difficult to see.

Cape Lopez region of Africa. They are peaceful and quite undemanding, being capable of adjusting to a variety of adverse conditions. A well-planted tank is recommended which receives subtle lighting and is supplied with well-aged water which is clean and clear with a slightly brownish tinge. The water should be soft, less than 10 DH, and somewhat acid, with a pH of 6.5 to 6.7, maintaining an average temperature between 72° and 75°F. They prefer live foods such as Daphnia, Tubifex worms and brine shrimp.

They reach a maximum length of about 2 inches and will start breeding at half that. The male is extremely handsome. His body is a dark brown which gives way to a yellow on the underside of the belly. The sides and central portion of the tail are jeweled with numerous irregular dots and dashes of a deep wine red. The fins are large and lovely. The tail is lyre-shaped with a purple border. It is tipped in white, while the center is blue. The female, in comparison, is washed out. Her body is a fawn or light brown with only a couple of red spots. Her fins are round compared to the long pointed flowing ones of the male.

They are willing breeders. Separate the sexes and condition the female on generous helpings of live foods until she is bulging with roe. Prepare a small bare breeding tank (1-3 gallons) at one end with a clump of fine-leaved plants *(Riccia, Utricularia, Nitella)* or a spawning mop. Set the aquarium temperature at about 75°F. and fill it with soft, acid water which will retard fungus growth. Since the male is such an active driver it is best to supply him with two to three females. Spawning takes place close to the surface where the eggs are laid singly and remain attached to the plants by fine adhesive threads. Spawning will continue over a number of days with 10 to 12

eggs being deposited each day. The parents usually don't eat their own eggs. After spawning drop the temperature down to 70°F. and darken the tank. The eggs have a relatively long period of development of 12 to 16 days, after which the fry are immediately free-swimming. The parents should then be removed.

Using the right kind of artificial spawning material can make retrieval of killie eggs convenient.

In the absence of floating plants, Lyretails can spawn at the bottom, too.

Supply the fry with newly hatched brine shrimp and sort and separate them by size.

Günther's Notho

Nothobranchius guentheri

The *Nothobranchius* species are mostly native to the eastern coast of Africa. They are small, brilliantly colored fishes which have adapted themselves to a most remarkable way of life. They range in bodies of water which usually dry up completely in the hot season. The eggs, which had been hastily buried in the bottom mud while the waters were receding, survive partial drying of the mud under the hot sun, and finally hatch when the rains again replenish the waterholes. They grow unbelievably fast and must

A male (colorful fish at the bottom) Günther's Notho and his female partner.

In nature this annual fish spawns in mud; in the aquarium other substrates will be used.

perpetuate their species before the drought again leaves them stranded.

In the aquarium they are best kept out of community tanks and given an uncrowded tank to themselves. *Nothobranchius guentheri* males are very attractively colored. The sides are a bright blue, with a dark border on each scale giving a reticulated effect. The dorsal fin is yellowish brown with dark rays, and the tail is a brilliant wine-red. The females are as drab as the males are beautiful. Their fins are shorter and uncolored, and the bodies

are a dirty gray with a few small black spots.

The males are eager spawners and ideally should be provided with 2 or even 3 females, as they have been known to drive a female long after she was depleted and bring on her untimely demise. We already know how they spawn in nature, but it would be highly impractical to have an aquarium with a mud bottom. Two things can be substituted: peat moss and fine sand. The water should be soft, about 5 DH, and the pH should be acid, about 6.5. Spawning temperature should be 76° to 78°F. A few plants can be floated, to give the female a place to hide if she is unduly harassed.

You will find that the female lays about 5 to 15 eggs each day for about 2 weeks, at which time there should never be a strong light on any part of the tank. The breeders do best with generous feedings of live foods.

After about two weeks, the breeders are netted out and the

water is removed from the tank very carefully. The tank is then covered and allowed to stand in a

The male is here pressing the female on the substrate where the eggs are deposited and fertilized.

semi-dry state for 3 months. The water is then replaced and if all goes well the eggs hatch in a very short time. At this time, the fry no longer have a yolk-sac attached and hunt for food at once. They are able to swallow newly-hatched brine shrimp immediately and grow with amazing speed if continuously supplied with this live food.

The fins of this female Günther's Notho are infected with Velvet, a disease caused by a freshwater protozoan parasite. This disease is very infectious, but sick fish can be treated and often recover.

White's Cynolebias

Cynolebias whitei

Members of this species are found in the shallow intermittent pools of the Rio Grande do Sul region in Brazil. They are annual fish. Their ponds dry up and disappear in the dry months. They have a very short life span and the whole of their life cycle: hatching, growth, spawning and dying all take place within a year.

They are often shy and do best if they are kept by themselves. They have hearty appetites and eat live or frozen food but they accept dry food only when they are famished. They must be fed constantly. The males reach about 3 inches; the females are somewhat smaller. Their water should be soft and neutral to slightly acid with a temperature between 72° and 76°F. They will do better if the water is made

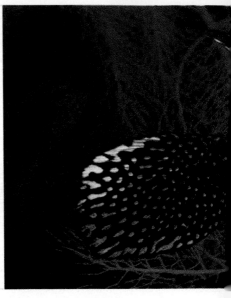

slightly brackish with a trace of salt.

They are quite lovely. They do not resemble other members of the genera in form, being longer, with flowing, highly pointed dorsal and anal fins. Their body is brownish with a number of shiny

A male and female White's Cynolebias pictured together, dramatically showing the characteristics of the male in contrast to those of the female.

bluish, greenish and golden dots arranged in symmetrical patterns. The fins of the male are reddish with blue dots, the anal fin is edged in blue and yellow which makes it appear green. The caudal fin is also tipped in green. The female is a drab olive green

A male Cynolebias whitei.

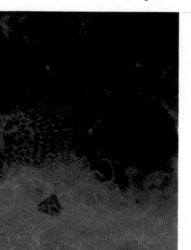

with a black patch on her side and another at her tail base.

They spawn in the manner typical of other *Cynolebias* and are prolific breeders, as are most annual fish. They will start breeding at 1½ inches when they are about six weeks old. They should be placed in a small tank of about 2½ to 5 gallons with several inches of fine sand or peat moss on the bottom. The male will swim over the bottom carefully inspecting it, looking for a suitable site; the female follows close behind. He will dip down, head first and the female will come into a position with her head between his body and pectoral fin. His pectoral fin is very sensitive. The male flips his tail and starts to make a hole in the bottom with his mouth. The pair will penetrate deep into the sediment until they almost disappear. With a rotating movement he flops onto his side and maneuvers the female down

so she is no longer visible; a single egg is deposited. The couple reappear and the egg is left buried under several inches of compost. This process will be repeated until all the eggs are depleted. Development requires 40 to 70 days to hatch. The water should be drained and only a little moisture allowed to remain. They should be stored at 75°F. After about six weeks the tank should be refilled with 2 or 3 inches of water. Within a few hours the fry will have hatched. They should be raised on newly hatched brine shrimp and microworms. Growth is rapid. Within two weeks the sexes can be distinguished by the red color of the male's fins and the black spot on the female.

Albino White's Cynolebias, a male and a female. Although the obvious differences in color are now muted, the characters of the sexes persist.

They are easily runted if not given ample room and a constant supply of live foods.

One interesting characteristic of this and certain other Killie species is the presence of tactile papillae on the first eight rays of the male's pectoral fins which indicate to him when the female is in position. They signal when to dive and when to turn over onto their sides.

Male White's Cynolebias.

The Siamese Fighting Fish

Betta splendens

The Betta, or Siamese fighting fish, is among the most famous of all aquarium fishes. From the original wild specimens that come from southeastern Asia have been bred many shades of long-finned beauties that could vie successfully in color and grace with many of our butterflies. The Thai natives, on the other hand, are a little more practical. Instead of breeding for lovely colors, they try to produce males that will fight bitterly when placed with another of their own sex. Such combats attract audiences of spectators who wager money on the outcome, and it is readily

Betta splendens.

understandable how the owner of a good battler could have himself a fairly valuable bit of property— for a time.

The Betta belongs to the Anabantid group, which has in common the possession of an auxiliary breathing organ known as a labyrinth. With the aid of this they come to the surface every few minutes for a gulp of atmospheric air from which they extract the oxygen into the blood stream. This renders the oxygen content of the water in which they are kept relatively unimportant, and makes it possible to raise many young fish in individual small jars where there is no danger that they will hurt each

Red Betta.

other. Dealers must also display male specimens in this manner, because putting two males together is of course the signal for a bitter fight which frequently results in one or both fish being damaged beyond repair. Females are more gregarious, and a number of them can be kept in the same aquarium.

Betta breeding is not very difficult. A pair consisting of an active, healthy male and a heavy-bodied female are placed in an aquarium where the water level has been reduced to six inches. This aquarium should have a normal capacity of 10 gallons or more. Here the low water level may pose a small problem. Heating such an aquarium with an ordinary thermostatically controlled heater which cannot be submerged cannot be done safely. To get around this, stand a

Cambodia Betta.

The Siamese Fighting Fish

jar filled with water which will hold the full length of the heater right into the tank. However, completely submersible heaters are now available. Keep the water temperature close to 80°F. A few sprigs of plants floating at the surface are an asset, and the bottom should be bare.

Now introduce your breeding pair. Put your male into the tank and place the female into a jar that floats in the water where he can see her. A glass partition can also be used temporarily. After a few hours, let the female out and watch what happens. The male may be a bit rough at first, and if

Red Betta.

the female is damaged she should be taken out for her own protection. Generally the male almost immediately begins to build a bubblenest. This is a group of bubbles he coats with saliva and may measure several inches across and three or four bubbles deep. During the bubblenest construction the female is chased away, but when the nest is finished there is a different attitude. Instead of chasing her away, he now tries to coax her into a position under the nest. Here he curls his body about hers in such a manner that their anal openings are close together. Amid a great deal of quivering a number of eggs are

discharged by the female and fertilized by the male. These eggs fall toward the bottom and the male hastens to pick them up in his mouth and spit them into the

Betta macrostoma.

bubblenest. This spawning act is repeated until the female is empty of eggs, at which time it is very advisable to remove her. The male now assumes great responsibility: the nest must be kept in repair, the eggs must be kept from falling out and a constant watch must be kept up for intruders.

In 24 to 30 hours at a temperature of 80°F. the eggs begin to hatch, and a mass of

Blue Betta.

tiny, quivering tails can be seen beneath the nest. The male gets even busier, because at this time more than ever the youngsters fall through the bubbles and must be spit back into the nest. The tiny

Separatory panels conveniently create compartments for isolating Bettas.

fry are very awkward and helpless at first, and it is not until 2 or 3 days later that the yolk sacs are absorbed and swimming is begun. Now the male really gets nervous, and his presence in the breeding aquarium is a menace rather than a help to the youngsters. Remove the male and isolate him in a 4-way breeding trap or floating jar.

Now comes the time when the youngsters must be fed. At first their mouths are tiny and Infusoria would be the perfect size, but not all hobbyists have the time and patience to prepare an Infusoria culture. Lacking this, the most finely pulverized dried foods can be used. An admirable substitute is the yolk of a hard-boiled chicken egg gathered into a clean square of cloth which is

held in the water and squeezed through the mesh little by little. Between feedings the cloth, yolk and all, is placed in the refrigerator. When the fry have grown a little, newly-hatched brine shrimp may be fed to them. The size of the belly is always an

A male and female Marble Betta, the male (on the right) apparently showing some interest in courting the female.

indication that the fish is eating his fill.

The water depth of six inches should be maintained for about 2 weeks, and then the water may be deepened an inch or two at a time until the tank is full. A cover must be kept on top at all times in

A male Betta with his just completed bubblenest.

This male Betta has started to release his partner and will soon be busy retrieving the fertilized eggs and depositing them in the bubblenest.

order to keep the air and water temperatures equal. A youngster that gets a mouthful of colder air every time he comes to the surface does not last long. A stream of bubbles from an airstone is also a necessity, to keep breaking up the oily film which would otherwise form on the surface.

Even with all these precautions

Male Bettas live compatibly with other fish species, but not with other male Bettas.

many fish will be lost: at about 3 weeks of age the newly-developed labyrinths begin to be put to use. At this stage of the game this organ is very sensitive, and in a few individuals it does not develop properly. These losses do not reflect on the skill of the breeder, they just happen.

Given proper conditions and feeding a Betta will attain its full size and development in 6 months. At a year they are at their prime.

As the fry get older, the bubblenest will slowly break up. The fry leaves the bubblenest, swims freely and starts to feed. Meanwhile the yolk sac becomes gradually smaller.

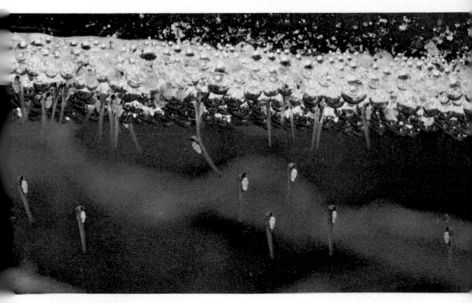

The Dwarf Gourami

Colisa lalia

The popular Dwarf Gouramis are native to the vegetation clogged rivers and streams of India, Bengal, and Assam. They are perfect aquarium fish since they are hardy, peaceful and quite undemanding. They have an elegant beauty but unfortunately tend to be shy when placed with aggressive species. Feeding presents little trouble since they will eagerly accept dried foods; however their diet should include occasional live supplements. They are members of the Anabantidae and possess the characteristic labyrinth which enables them to breath atmospheric oxygen.

C. lalia are the smallest of their genus. The males never exceed 2½ inches and the female 2 inches. They are beautiful. The body of the male, which is oval and compressed laterally, is adorned with alternating series of shiny blue-green and red stripes which are also present, although irregular, in the unpaired fins. The dorsal is red with blue dots, while the anal and caudal fins are orange with blue dots and dashes. The elongated extensions of the second rays of the ventrals are an orange-red and are generously provided with sense

The male and female Dwarf Gourami have the same color pattern, but the male coloration is much more intense.

organs. The throat and belly are indigo. The female is paler, her body a grayish silver with delicate blue stripes. Her fins are translucent and the dorsal, anal and caudal fins are bordered with red and sprinkled with red flecks. Her throat and belly are bluish white.

A suitable artificial environment for these fish would include a small tank which is well stocked with floating aquatic plants and receives a generous amount of sunlight. A dark bottom is recommended, since it shows their lovely colors off to best advantage. Normal tap water, which varies from neutral to slightly acid, may be used. Aeration is not essential because

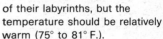

A male Dwarf Gourami wrapped around the female beneath the bubblenest.

of their labyrinths, but the temperature should be relatively warm (75° to 81° F.).

When you attempt to breed this species, choose a healthy pair which are not more than a year old, and condition them on choice live foods until the female is full and the male is even more handsomely colored. In the evening place the male in a ten gallon well-planted breeding tank which is filled with six inches of water which has been aged about a day. The tank should be placed so that it receives large quantities of sunshine to encourage the growth of algae. The male will begin to build a bubblenest. The female should be introduced early the next morning and may help finish the nest. This species employs bits of vegetation-leaves, twigs and roots, as framework for the nest, forming a compact mass. When complete, it is

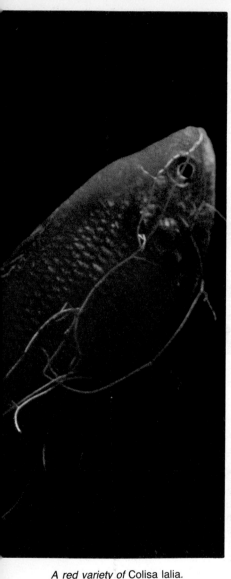

embrace under the nest. With his body encircling the female, he maneuvers her into an upside down position with her abdomen directed toward the surface. Eggs are released and fertilized as they float aimlessly toward the surface. The male relaxes his embrace and quickly gathers the eggs and carefully places them into the nest. Spawning is continued at frequent intervals until the female is exhausted of her store of eggs and then she is driven away. The male attends the nest alone. The tiny eggs usually number about 100 to 150 and hatch in about two days. The fry are free-swimming in two more days and should be fed small Infusoria. They are quite small and delicate at first and many starve.

Very young Dwarf Gourami fry, less than two hours after hatching.

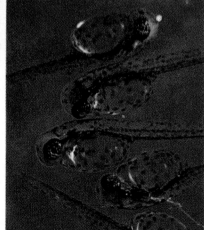

A red variety of Colisa lalia. *Strands of water plants are often included in building the bubblenest.*

several inches in diameter and often extends above the surface of the water.

The male proudly spreads his fins and the pair enter into an

The Paradise Fish

Everything about a male Paradise Fish is impressive, his coloration, the size of the fins and his temperament.

Macropodus opercularis

The Paradise Fish are native to the stagnant, muddy streams and rice paddies of Southern China and Formosa. There are numerous opinions as to their disposition; although they can occasionally live in harmony with other fishes, they are perpetually hostile toward their own kind and have an undesirable habit of making sudden lunges at members of their own species, butting rather than nipping them. They are able to adjust to extremes in temperature from 50° to 90°F. and should be kept in an unheated aquarium or an outdoor pool during the warmer months. High temperatures tend to shorten their life. They seem to do best at around 65° to 70°F.; 70° to 75°F. is sufficient for breeding.

They have enormous appetites and should be fed copious amounts of food. They are full grown at about 3 inches but will start breeding at 2½ inches. They are quite handsomely colored. A brownish green background is transversed with alternating dark blue and red metallic bands. The fins are blue with light stripes. The tail, which is red with green bands and dotted with blue spots, is forked into two long blue filaments. The dorsal is large and blue with white margin and spots. The anal fin is blue anteriorly becoming red posteriorly. The sexes are difficult to distinguish before maturity. The male is the more aggressive with deeper coloration and larger fins. He is especially gorgeous at breeding time when he sports red, peacock blue, orange and emerald green in tasteful combinations. The female is duller having only the red transverse bands. There are three color variations of this species: red, black and albino. The albino is the more peaceful.

They are quite undemanding make use of atmospheric air.

Prior to breeding divide a four to five gallon aquarium (which contains numerous bushy plants) with a glass partition. Condition for several days on foods such as brine shrimp and Tubifex worms. Spawning can easily be induced

Like a true Anabantoid, the Paradise Fish builds a bubblenest.

An artist's illustration of Paradise Fish.

by raising the temperature. Since the males have mean tempers, no more than one pair should share an aquarium. Remove the partition only when the female is swollen and ready for spawning or the male may badly mutilate her. The plants are present to provide her with hiding places if the driving becomes too strenuous. The male may often build a bubble nest which he anchors to the floating plants. He will try to entice the female under his nest by displaying his magnificent colors and spreading his gill-plates wide. They come into close contact with their fins fully spread vibrating their bodies against one another. The male swishes his ventrals back and

and will live in dirty, muddy water. This is possible since they can

An albino Paradise Fish loses all the dark pigments but not the red pigments that are still visible in the body bands, fins and eyes.

forth which rotates the pair slowly. Then he completely encircles his mate with his body and when she is in an upside down position he helps squeeze the eggs out. He slips from the embrace, gathers the eggs carefully in his mouth and blows them into the nest. After mating, the female should be removed. The male becomes a conscientious parent and takes on the task of raising the young. During this time he retains his brilliant hues and is most hostile.

The numerous small white eggs will hatch in 30 to 50 hours. The father will catch the young fry and blow them back into the nest until their yolk sacs are completely absorbed and they are free-swimming. The male should then be removed. The fry are easy to raise but overcrowding will stunt their growth. They should be fed small particles of food such as Infusoria and newly hatched brine shrimp. The nursery tank should have a tightly fitting cover since the fry are extremely sensitive to chills at this stage.

The Three Spot or Blue Gourami

Three-spot Gourami, a specimen showing the characters of the wild type.

which lies on nearly the same line as the other two. There are several pale pink spots on the fins. The sexes are similar in appearance, except the males have larger dorsal and anal fins. During the breeding season the males develop a deep midnight blue color. The females acquire a darker color also. They make a very handsome pair.

Choose a breeding tank which is large and long, about 20 gallons, with a fair number of aquatics to provide protection for the female. These fish breed readily. In the morning the male can be seen busily at work constructing a bubblenest which

The Cosby strain of the Three-spot Gourami is also very popular.

Trichogaster trichopterus
Three Spot Gouramis from the tropical Far East are robust, prolific, and more hardy and aggressive than most Gouramis. They reach an average length of 5 inches and will begin breeding at 3½ inches. They should only be kept with other fishes of approximately the same size. Water requirements are flexible; temperatures between 70° and 88° F. are quite suitable. They have hearty appetites and accept any freeze-dried or live aquarium food; they are useful for ridding tanks of the dreaded *Hydra* which they find a delicacy.

Their body is silver blue with a series of incomplete blue bars on the posterior portion of the body. There are two black spots, one on the center of the body, the other on the caudal peduncle. The common name includes the eye

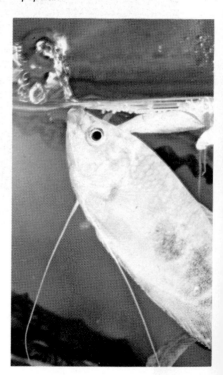

may employ some of the leaves of the floating aquatic plants. It is a hodgepodge of scattered bubbles indiscriminately placed. When he has finished, he attempts to lure the female under, often butting her in the abdomen. When they

A golden variety of the Three-spot Gourami. This is a male guarding his bubblenest.

and carefully places them into the nest. Spawning may continue over several hours, after which the female should be removed. They are quite prolific and the average brood numbers almost a thousand. The male keeps watch over the nest, mouthing the eggs occasionally and rearranging them. The eggs hatch in about 30 hours and soon after the colors of the male begin to fade. He should

are beneath the nest he wraps his body around her and rolls her over so that her belly is directed towards the surface. After much trembling the eggs are released and fertilized. The eggs are lighter than water so they rise to the surface. The female is released and the male gathers the eggs

be removed when the fry are free-swimming. The water level should be lowered to about 6 inches and a cover placed over the tank. The fry should be given Infusoria and brine shrimp nauplii. The third week is the critical period of development, while the labyrinth is developing.

The Guppy

Poecilia reticulata

Guppies are so readily available, inexpensive, and easy to keep and breed that inevitably they become recommended first fish for almost all beginning aquarists. The Guppy, along with the Platies, Mollies and Swordtails, belongs to the family Poeciliidae and, except for one subfamily, all poeciliids are livebearers. As such they are interesting fishes and have been the subject of a vast amount of experiments and research. Due to its voracious appetite for insect larvae, the Guppy has been utilized as a means of controlling mosquitoes.

economy medium sized tanks (10-20 gallons) are adequate. Crowding can inhibit growth but too few fish in a large tank is wasteful.

Like most fishes dependent on gill respiration (labyrinth fishes are able to obtain oxygen from the atmosphere), the amount of available oxygen in the water is critical. Aeration plays an important role particularly in a densely populated tank. Overfeeding, which is so common among beginners, can result in fouling the water and lead to oxygen depletion. Excess food together with other detrital

The Guppy originated in the fresh and brackish streams of northern Brazil, Guyana, Venezuela and in the islands of Barbados and Trinidad. Through the years it has been introduced in many areas, and they are now known existing in the wilds of every temperate and tropical continent of the world.

In temperate areas Guppies can pass winter even in an unheated tank as low as 65° F., but they may fail to survive temperatures lower than 50° F. A water temperature between 68° and 80° F. is satisfactory for keeping and breeding fancy Guppies. For convenience and

Representatives of the wild type of Guppy. A larger female, along with 2 smaller males.

accumulations should always be removed periodically. Overcrowding should be avoided. A lesser number of healthy fish is much better than an excess of sick and dying Guppies.

Water hardness is not critical, but extreme amounts of minerals are not desirable. Water of medium hardness (6-10 DH) is recommended. Guppies inhabit brackish water in the wild and may even survive in sea water

One of the many Guppy varieties developed is the snakeskin, called such on account of the reticulated body pattern.

provided the transition is gradual, though the addition of salt water even if introduced gradually is not wise. The best salinity range is between 500 to 1,000 parts per million. The addition of a level teaspoon of rock salt to a gallon of tap water roughly produces a salinity of 1,000 parts per million. A pH between 6.5 and 7.0 is reasonable for any Guppy. Again extremes are best avoided.

Guppies are omnivorous; they eat both animal and plant food. The natural animal food is mostly insect larvae and crustaceans. They are quite happy with Tubifex, Artemia, Daphnia, Cyclops and mosquito larvae and they accept dry food also. To complete the diet choppped spinach or other vegetable material may be given. Freeze-dried foods are a real treat. Without doubt Guppies can be kept in a bare tank

This large female Guppy is more colorful than a normal female due to hormone treatment.

Closeup of the gonopodium, the male copulatory organ.

satisfactorily, but the presence of a gravel substrate, some plants and a few rocks or stones provides a more natural setting than a bare aquarium.

Just like any other species one selects the parents with care. There are many varieties of domesticated Guppies available commercially from fancy Guppy breeders, pet shops or from members of Guppy associations. The selection is so wide that choice is only limited by personal preference. The males of both the wild and domesticated forms are

much smaller and more colorful than the females. The females of earlier stocks of Guppies were even less colorful. However, through selection and breeding, and in some cases by hormone treatment, colorful females were produced. Males are easily identified by the presence of the gonopodium or copulatory organ found in most livebearers.

With a separating glass panel one can conserve tank space and at the same time isolate and precondition the selected female (preferably a previously unmated

Heterandria formosa is another Poeciliid, also with gonopodium, shown here ready for mating.

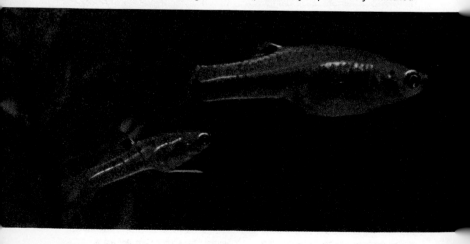

or virgin fish) and male prior to spawning in the same tank.

Courtship in Guppies is an elaborate affair with the male performing the greater role. When both males and females are kept together, the males are mostly occupied chasing and courting the females, in constant search

Extreme development of the gonopodium in some domesticated Guppy strains is a great disadvantage to breeding. Such a gonopodium is incapable of normal function.

soon makes a loop by swimming behind her and turning back below her abdominal region to effect a contact between his extended gonopodium and her genital pore. Normally the gonopodium is directed backward, but during mating it is pointed forward. In association with some pelvic fin rays it forms a groove through which the spermatophore (a compact bundle of sperm cells) is introduced into the genital opening of the female. The tip of the gonopodium also bears hooks to ensure penetration and

for a willing female. One can expect the same type of activity in a pair of Guppies intended for breeding. The male approaches the female from behind and he chases her for some time until he confronts her, pausing directly in front of her. Then he turns away from her but at the same time makes S-shaped motions as if to hold her attention further. If receptive, she follows him and keeps on swimming until they are parallel to each other. Then the male positions himself transversely before her and displays some more by extending his tail fin; his spots and body color appear more intense. He

attachment for a few seconds. Copulation is not always successful, so the courtship ritual is repeated several times. A successful contact lasts about 5 seconds. Out of hundreds of "passes," successful copulations may number less than ten! The male can be removed after the mating.

The sperm cells are retained in the folds of the genital tract of the female and several successive monthly batches of eggs can be fertilized, resulting in a succession of broods. For this reason it is not wise to use more than one male at one time or to mate the same female to a different male too soon. Using only virgin females precludes getting fry of unknown male parentage.

Depending on the temperature and other conditions such as light and food, the gestation period lasts about 4 to 6 weeks. Females in the last stages of pregnancy should be handled carefully. She could drop her young prematurely and can be fatally hurt. Relative to her size and age, a female Guppy can give birth to a brood of 20 to 100 fry or in rare cases even 200. They are released still encased by a delicate membrane which is removed as the fry uncoils immediately upon release or seconds later as it drops down toward the bottom. Sometimes within two-minute time intervals three fish are born. They swim actively and, being phototropic, will move toward the most lighted part of the tank. They start feeding immediately.

A group of developing Guppy embryos surgically removed from a pregnant female prior to birth.

A female Guppy dropping her live young, still encased in a membrane.

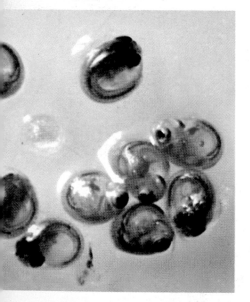

Unfortunately, they can become the food of the mother or any other fish in the tank. A good plant cover of *Nitella, Myriophyllum* and other fine-leafed plants provides a barrier which is not only effective but natural in appearance also. The fry can easily go through a dense mass of plants where the adult is unable to pursue them.

When all the fish in a litter are released the female can be removed and one can expect the next brood to emerge 30 days later at a temperature of 75° F. under good lighting and food conditions.

The young can be fed newly-hatched brine shrimp and microworms together with a mixture of powdered dried foods. They can be kept in a 10- or 20-gallon aquarium for a month or so. They grow rapidly and are sexually mature in two months but reach full growth in six months. As soon as they are sexable, segregate them according to sex to prevent early matings. Only full-grown fish should be mated.

Suggested Reading

The following books published by T.F.H. Publications are available at pet shops and book stores everywhere.

Dr. Axelrod's Atlas of Freshwater Aquarium Fishes
By Dr. Herbert R. Axelrod, Dr. Warren E. Burgess, Neal Pronek, and Jerry G. Walls.
ISBN 0-86622-052-6
T.F.H. H-1077
The ultimate aquarium book—illustrated with over 4000 color photos. Almost every fish available to hobbyists is illustrated! Species are grouped geographically and by family for easy reference. No aquarist's library is complete without it!

Exotic Tropical Fishes Expanded Edition
By Dr. Herbert R. Axelrod, Dr. C. W. Emmens, Dr. Warren E. Burgess, and Neal Pronek.
ISBN 0-87666-543-1 (hardcover),
ISBN 0-87666-537-7 (looseleaf)
T.F.H. H-1028 (hardcover),
H-1028L (looseleaf)
The "bible" of freshwater ornamental fishes—contains comprehensive information on aquarium maintenance, plants, and commercial culture, as well as over 1,000 color photos and entries on many hundreds of species. New supplements are issued every month in *Tropical Fish Hobbyist* magazine, and may be placed into the looseleaf edition.

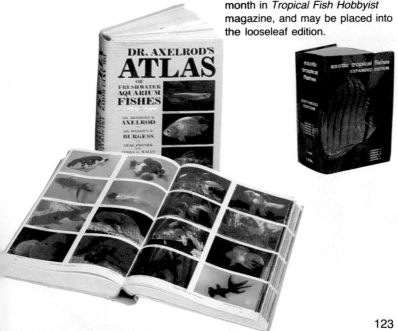

Index

A school of Harlequins (*Rasbora heteromorpha*).

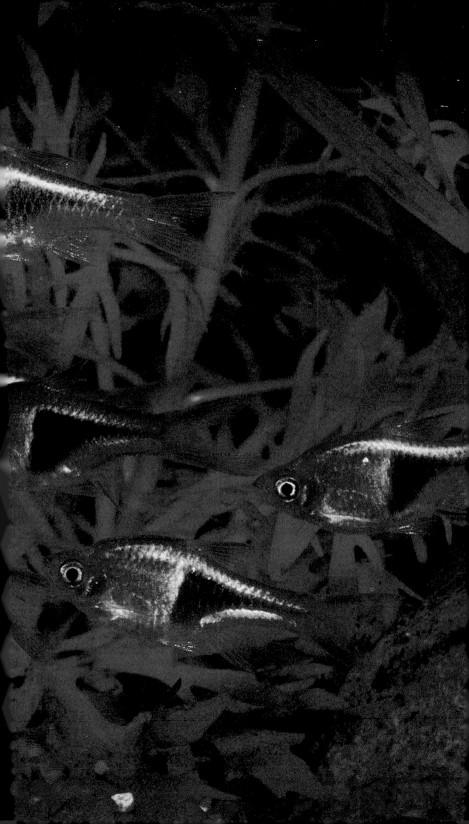

CO-007 S

A COMPLETE INTRODUCTION TO

BREEDING
AQUARIUM FISHES

A male Three-spined Stickleback (Gasterosteus aculeatus) mouthing and cleaning the eggs in the nest that he constructed earlier.